The Pleasures Of Life, Complete

You are holding a reproduction of an original work that is in the public domain in the United States of America, and possibly other countries. You may freely copy and distribute this work as no entity (individual or corporate) has a copyright on the body of the work. This book may contain prior copyright references, and library stamps (as most of these works were scanned from library copies). These have been scanned and retained as part of the historical artifact.

This book may have occasional imperfections such as missing or blurred pages, poor pictures, errant marks, etc. that were either part of the original artifact, or were introduced by the scanning process. We believe this work is culturally important, and despite the imperfections, have elected to bring it back into print as part of our continuing commitment to the preservation of printed works worldwide. We appreciate your understanding of the imperfections in the preservation process, and hope you enjoy this valuable book.

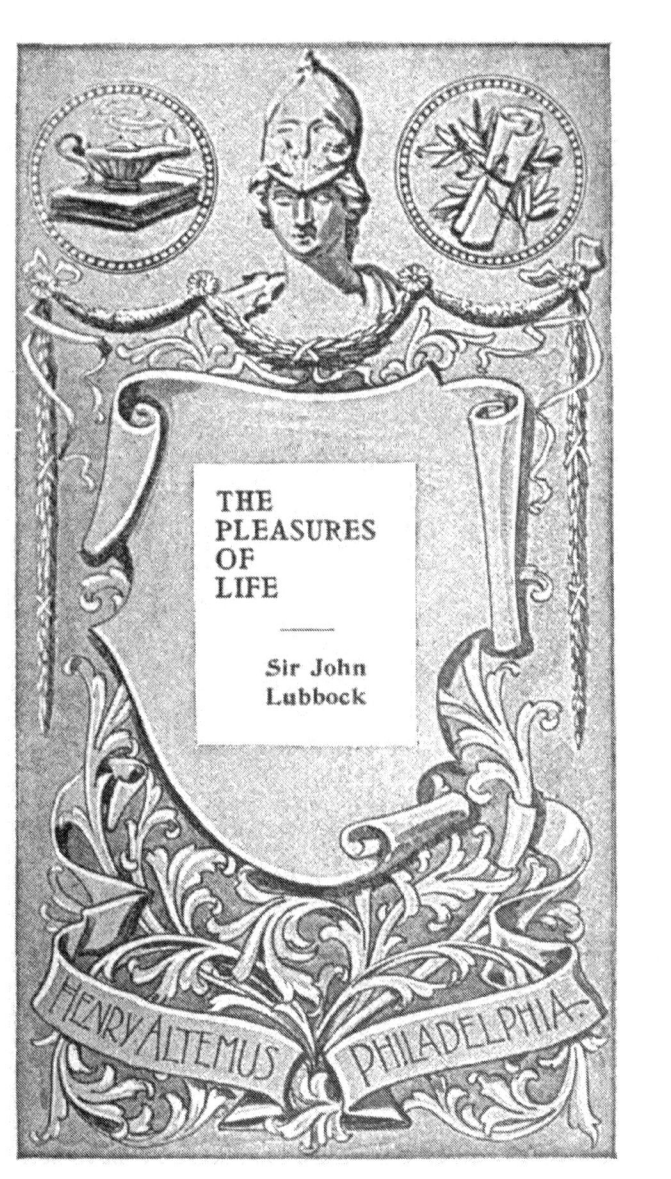

THE
PLEASURES OF LIFE

COMPLETE.

BY

THE RIGHT HON.
SIR JOHN LUBBOCK, BART., M.P.

F.R.S., D.C.L., LL.D.

PRESIDENT OF THE LONDON CHAMBER OF COMMERCE
PRINCIPAL OF THE LONDON WORKING-MEN'S COLLEGE
AND
CHAIRMAN OF THE LONDON COUNTY COUNCIL

PHILADELPHIA
HENRY ALTEMUS
1895

KC 2719

ALTEMUS'
BOOKBINDERY
PHILADELPHIA

CONTENTS.

PART I

CHAPTER I
                                        PAGE
THE DUTY OF HAPPINESS 1

CHAPTER II
THE HAPPINESS OF DUTY 20

CHAPTER III
A SONG OF BOOKS 36

CHAPTER IV
THE CHOICE OF BOOKS 48

CHAPTER V
THE BLESSING OF FRIENDS 64

CHAPTER VI

The Value of Time 73

CHAPTER VII

The Pleasures of Travel 81

CHAPTER VIII

The Pleasures of Home 94

CHAPTER IX

Science 103

CHAPTER X

Education 121

PART II

CHAPTER I

Ambition 139

CHAPTER II

Wealth 151

CONTENTS.

CHAPTER III
	PAGE
HEALTH	159

CHAPTER IV
LOVE	175

CHAPTER V
ART	191

CHAPTER VI
POETRY	207

CHAPTER VII
MUSIC	221

CHAPTER VIII
THE BEAUTIES OF NATURE	237

CHAPTER IX
THE TROUBLES OF LIFE	261

CHAPTER X
LABOR AND REST	273

CHAPTER XI
RELIGION	283

CHAPTER XII

THE HOPE OF PROGRESS 301

CHAPTER XIII.

THE DESTINY OF MAN 315

PREFACE.

THOSE who have the pleasure of attending the opening meetings of schools and colleges, and of giving away prizes and certificates, are generally expected at the same time to offer such words of counsel and encouragement as the experience of the world might enable them to give to those who are entering life.

Having been myself when young rather prone to suffer from low spirits, I have at several of these gatherings taken the opportunity of dwelling on the privileges and blessings we enjoy, and I reprint here the substance of some of these addresses (omitting what was special to the circumstances of each case, and freely making any alterations and additions which have since occurred to me), hoping that the thoughts and quotations in which I have myself found most comfort may perhaps be of use to others also.

It is hardly necessary to say that I have not by

any means referred to all the sources of happiness open to us, some indeed of the greatest pleasures and blessings being altogether omitted.

In reading over the proofs I feel that some sentences may appear too dogmatic, but I hope that allowance will be made for the circumstances under which they were delivered.

HIGH ELMS,
DOWN, KENT, *January* 1887.

PREFACE

TO THE TWENTIETH EDITION.

A LECTURE which I delivered three years ago at the Working Men's College, and which forms the fourth chapter of this book, has given rise to a good deal of discussion. The *Pall Mall Gazette* took up the subject and issued a circular to many of those best qualified to express an opinion. This elicited many interesting replies, and some other lists of books were drawn up. When my book was translated, a similar discussion took place in Germany. The result has been very gratifying, and after carefully considering the suggestions which have been made, I see no reason for any material change in the first list. I had not presumed to form a list of my own, nor did I profess to give my own favorites. My attempt was to give those most generally recommended by previous writers on the subject. In the various criticisms on my list, while large additions, amounting to several hundred works in all, have been proposed, very few omissions have been suggested. As regards those works with reference to which some doubts have been expressed—namely, the few Oriental books, Wake's Apostolic Fathers, etc.—I may observe that I drew up the list, not as that of the hundred best books, but, which is very different, of those which have been most frequently recommended as best worth reading.

For instance as regards the *Sheking* and the *Analects* of Confucius, I must humbly confess that I do not greatly admire either; but I recommended them because they are held in the most profound veneration by the Chinese race, containing 400,000,000 of our fellow-men. I may add that both works are quite short.

The *Ramayana* and *Maha Bharata* (as epitomized by Wheeler) and St. Hilaire's *Bouddha* are not only very interesting in themselves, but very important in reference to our great oriental Empire.

The authentic writings of the Apostolic Fathers are very short, being indeed comprised in one small volume, and as the only works (which have come down to us) of those who lived with and knew the Apostles, they are certainly well worth reading.

I have been surprised at the great divergence of opinion which has been expressed. Nine lists of some length have been published. These lists contain some three hundred works not mentioned by me (without, however, any corresponding omissions), and yet there is not one single book which occurs in every list, or even in half of them, and only about half a dozen which appear in more than one of the nine.

If these authorities, or even a majority of them, had concurred in their recommendations, I would have availed myself of them; but as they differ so greatly I will allow my list to remain almost as I first proposed it. I have, however, added Kalidasa's *Sakuntala* or *The Lost Ring*, and Schiller's *William Tell*, omitting, in consequence, Lucretius and Miss Austen: Lucretius because though his work is most remarkable, it is perhaps less generally suitable than most of the others in the list; and Miss Austen because English novelists were somewhat over-represented.

High Elms,
Down, Kent, *August* 1890.

THE PLEASURES OF LIFE

PART I

"All places that the eye of Heaven visits
  Are to the wise man ports and happy havens."

                              SHAKESPEARE.

"Some murmur, when their sky is clear
    And wholly bright to view,
  If one small speck of dark appear
    In their great heaven of blue.
  And some with thankful love are fill'd
    If but one streak of light,
  One ray of God's good mercy gild
    The darkness of their night.

"In palaces are hearts that ask,
    In discontent and pride,
  Why life is such a dreary task,
    And all good things denied.
  And hearts in poorest huts admire
    How love has in their aid
  (Love that not ever seems to tire)
    Such rich provision made."

                              TRENCH.

CHAPTER I.

THE DUTY OF HAPPINESS.

"If a man is unhappy, this must be his own fault; for God made all men to be happy."—Epictetus.

LIFE is a great gift, and as we reach years of discretion, we most of us naturally ask ourselves what should be the main object of our existence. Even those who do not accept "the greatest good of the greatest number" as an absolute rule, will yet admit that we should all endeavor to contribute as far as we may to the happiness of our fellow-creatures. There are many, however, who seem to doubt whether it is right that we should try to be happy ourselves. Our own happiness ought not, of course, to be our main object, nor indeed will it ever be secured if selfishly sought. We may have many pleasures in life, but must not let them have rule over us, or they will soon hand us over to sorrow; and "into what dangerous and miserable servitude doth he fall who suffereth pleasures and sorrows (two unfaithful and cruel commanders) to possess him successively?"[1]

I cannot, however, but think that the world would be better and brighter if our teachers would dwell on the Duty of Happiness as well as on the Happiness of Duty; for we ought to be as cheerful as we can, if only because to be happy ourselves, is a most effectual contribution to the happiness of others.

Every one must have felt that a cheerful friend is like a sunny day, which sheds its brightness on all around; and most of us can, as we choose, make of this world either a palace or a prison.

There is no doubt some selfish satisfaction in yielding to melancholy, and fancying that we are victims of fate; in brooding over grievances, especially if more or less imaginary. To be bright and cheerful often requires an effort; there is a certain art in keeping ourselves happy: and in this respect, as in others, we require to watch over and manage ourselves, almost as if we were somebody else.

Sorrow and joy, indeed, are strangely interwoven. Too often

> "We look before and after,
> And pine for what is not:
> Our sincerest laughter
> With some pain is fraught;
> Our sweetest songs are those that tell of saddest thought."[2]

[1] Seneca. [2] Shelley.

As a nation we are prone to melancholy. It has been said of our countrymen that they take even their pleasures sadly. But this, if it be true at all, will, I hope, prove a transitory characteristic. "Merry England" was the old saying, let us hope it may become true again. We must look to the East for real melancholy. What can be sadder than the lines with which Omar Khayyam opens his quatrains: [1]

> "We sojourn here for one short day or two,
> And all the gain we get is grief and woe;
> And then, leaving life's problems all unsolved
> And harassed by regrets, we have to go;"

or the Devas' song to Prince Siddârtha, in Edwin Arnold's beautiful version:

> "We are the voices of the wandering wind,
> Which moan for rest, and rest can never find.
> Lo! as the wind is, so is mortal life—
> A moan, a sigh, a sob, a storm, a strife."

If indeed this be true, if mortal life be so sad and full of suffering, no wonder that Nirvâna—the cessation of sorrow—should be welcomed even at the sacrifice of consciousness.

But ought we not to place before ourselves a very different ideal—a healthier, manlier, and nobler hope?

Life is not to live merely, but to live well.

[1] I quote from Whinfield's translation.

There are some "who live without any design at all, and only pass in the world like straws on a river: they do not go; they are carried,"[1]—but as Homer makes Ulysses say, "How dull it is to pause, to make an end, to rest unburnished; not to shine in use—as though to breathe were life!"

Goethe tells us that at thirty he resolved "to work out life no longer by halves, but in all its beauty and totality."

> "Im Ganzen, Guten, Schönen
> Resolut zu leben."

Life indeed must be measured by thought and action, not by time. It certainly may be, and ought to be, bright, interesting, and happy; and, according to the Italian proverb, "if all cannot live on the Piazza, every one may feel the sun."

If we do our best; if we do not magnify trifling troubles; if we look resolutely, I do not say at the bright side of things, but at things as they really are; if we avail ourselves of the manifold blessings which surround us; we cannot but feel that life is indeed a glorious inheritance.

> "More servants wait on man
> Than he'll take notice of. In every path
> He treads down that which doth befriend him
> When sickness makes him pale and wan
> Oh mighty Love! Man is one world, and hath
> Another to attend him."[2]

[1] Seneca.   [2] Herbert.

Few of us, however, realize the wonderful privilege of living, or the blessings we inherit; the glories and beauties of the Universe, which is our own if we choose to have it so; the extent to which we can make ourselves what we wish to be; or the power we possess of securing peace, of triumphing over pain and sorrow.

Dante pointed to the neglect of opportunities as a serious fault:

> "Man can do violence
> To himself and his own blessings, and for this
> He, in the second round, must aye deplore,
> With unavailing penitence, his crime.
> Whoe'er deprives himself of life and light
> In reckless lavishment his talent wastes,
> And sorrows then when he should dwell in joy."

Ruskin has expressed this with special allusion to the marvellous beauty of this glorious world, too often taken as a matter of course, and remembered, if at all, almost without gratitude. "Holy men," he complains, "in the recommending of the love of God to us, refer but seldom to those things in which it is most abundantly and immediately shown; though they insist much on His giving of bread, and raiment, and health (which He gives to all inferior creatures): they require us not to thank Him for that glory of His works which He has permitted us alone to perceive: they tell us often to meditate in the closet, but they send us not, like Isaac, into the fields at even: they dwell on the duty of self denial, but they exhibit not the duty of delight:" and yet, as he justly says elsewhere, "each of us, as we travel the way of life, has the choice, according to our working, of turning all the voices of Nature into one song of rejoicing; or of withering and quenching her sympathy into a fearful withdrawn silence of condemnation,—into a crying out of her stones and a shaking of her dust against us."

Must we not all admit, with Sir Henry Taylor, that "the retrospect of life swarms with lost opportunities"? "Whoever enjoys not life," says Sir T. Browne, "I count him but an apparition, though he wears about him the visible affections of flesh."

St. Bernard, indeed, goes so far as to maintain that "nothing can work me damage except myself; the harm that I sustain I carry about with me, and never am a real sufferer but by my own fault."

Some Heathen moralists also have taught very much the same lesson. "The gods," says Marcus Aurelius, "have put all the means in man's power to enable him not to fall into real evils. Now that which does not make a man worse, how can it make his life worse?"

Epictetus takes the same line: "If a man is unhappy, remember that his unhappiness is his own fault; for God has made all men to be happy." "I am," he elsewhere says, "always content with that which happens; for I think that what God chooses is better than what I choose." And again: "Seek not that things should happen as you wish; but wish the things which happen to be as they are, and you will have a tranquil flow of life. . . . If you wish for anything which belongs to another, you lose that which is your own."

Few, however, if any, can I think go as far as St. Bernard. We cannot but suffer from pain, sickness, and anxiety; from the loss, the unkindness, the faults, even the coldness of those we love. How many a day has been damped and darkened by an angry word!

Hegel is said to have calmly finished his *Phaenomenologie des Geistes* at Jena, on the 14th October 1806, not knowing anything whatever of the battle that was raging round him.

Matthew Arnold has suggested that we might take a lesson from the heavenly bodies.

> "Unaffrighted by the silence round them,
>   Undistracted by the sights they see,
> These demand not the things without them
>   Yield them love, amusement, sympathy.
>
> Bounded by themselves, and unobservant
>   In what state God's other works may be,
> In their own tasks all their powers pouring,
>   These attain the mighty life you see."

It is true that

> "A man is his own star;
>   Our acts our angels are
>   For good or ill,"

and that "rather than follow a multitude to do evil," one should "stand like Pompey's pillar, conspicuous by oneself, and single in integrity." [1] But to many this isolation would be itself most painful, for the heart is "no island cut off from other lands, but a continent that joins to them." [2]

If we separate ourselves so much from the interests of those around us that we do not sympathize with them in their sufferings, we shut ourselves out from sharing their happiness, and lose far more than we gain. If we avoid sympathy and wrap ourselves round in a cold chain armor of selfishness, we exclude ourselves from many of the greatest and purest joys of life. To render ourselves insensible to pain we must forfeit also the possibility of happiness.

Moreover, much of what we call evil is really good in disguise, and we should not "quarrel rashly with adversities not yet understood, nor overlook the mercies often bound up in them." [3] Pleasure and pain are, as Plutarch says, the nails which fasten body and soul together. Pain is a warning of danger, a very necessity of existence. But for it, but for the warnings which our feelings give us, the very blessings by which we are surrounded would soon and inevitably prove fatal. Many of those who have not studied the question are under the impression that the more deeply-seated portions of the body must be most sensitive. The very reverse is the case. The skin is a con-

[1] Sir T. Browne. [2] Bacon. [3] Sir T. Browne.

tinuous and ever-watchful sentinel, always on guard to give us notice of any approaching danger; while the flesh and inner organs, where pain would be without purpose, are, so long as they are in health, comparatively without sensation.

"We talk," says Helps, "of the origin of evil; . . . but what is evil? We mostly speak of sufferings and trials as good, perhaps, in their result; but we hardly admit that they may be good in themselves. Yet they are knowledge—how else to be acquired, unless by making men as gods, enabling them to understand without experience. All that men go through may be absolutely the best for them—no such thing as evil, at least in our customary meaning of the word."

Indeed, "the vale best discovereth the hill," [1] and "pour sentir les grands biens, il faut qu'il connoisse les petits maux."[2]

But even if we do not seem to get all that we should wish, many will feel, as in Leigh Hunt's beautiful translation of Filicaja's sonnet, that—

> "So Providence for us, high, infinite,
> Makes our necessities its watchful task,
> Hearkens to all our prayers, helps all our wants,
> And e'en if it denies what seems our right,
> Either denies because 'twould have us ask,
> Or seems but to deny, and in denying grants."

Those on the other hand who do not accept the idea of continual interferences, will rejoice in the

[1] Bacon. [2] Rousseau.

belief that on the whole the laws of the Universe work out for the general happiness.

And if it does come—

> " Grief should be
> Like joy, majestic, equable, sedate,
> Confirming, cleansing, raising, making free:
> Strong to consume small troubles; to commend
> Great thoughts, grave thoughts, thoughts lasting to the end." [1]

If, however, we cannot hope that life will be all happiness, we may at least secure a heavy balance on the right side; and even events which look like misfortune, if boldly faced, may often be turned to good. Oftentimes, says Seneca, "calamity turns to our advantage; and great ruins make way for greater glories." Helmholtz dates his start in science to an attack of illness. This led to his acquisition of a microscope, which he was enabled to purchase, owing to his having spent his autumn vacation of 1841 in the hospital, prostrated by typhoid fever; being a pupil, he was nursed without expense, and on his recovery he found himself in possession of the savings of his small resources.

"Savonarola," says Castelar, "would, under different circumstances, undoubtedly have been a good husband, a tender father; a man unknown to history, utterly powerless to print upon the sands of time and upon the human soul the deep trace

[1] Aubrey de Vere.

which he has left; but misfortune came to visit him, to crush his heart, and to impart that marked melancholy which characterizes a soul in grief; and the grief that circled his brows with a crown of thorns was also that which wreathed them with the splendor of immortality. His hopes were centered in the woman he loved, his life was set upon the possession of her, and when her family finally rejected him, partly on account of his profession, and partly on account of his person, he believed that it was death that had come upon him, when in truth it was immortality."

It is, however, impossible to deny the existence of evil, and the reason for it has long exercised the human intellect. The Savage solves it by the supposition of evil Spirits. The Greeks attributed the misfortunes of men in great measure to the antipathies and jealousies of gods and goddesses. Others have imagined two divine principles, opposite and antagonistic—the one friendly, the other hostile, to men.

Freedom of action, however, seems to involve the existence of evil. If any power of selection be left us, much must depend on the choice we make. In the very nature of things, two and two cannot make five. Epictetus imagines Jupiter addressing man as follows: "If it had been possible to make your body and your property free from liability to injury, I would have done so. As this could not be, I have given you a small portion of myself."

This divine gift it is for us to use wisely. It is, in fact, our most valuable treasure. "The soul is a much better thing than all the others which you possess. Can you then show me in what way you have taken care of it? For it is not likely that you, who are so wise a man, inconsiderately and carelessly allow the most valuable thing that you possess to be neglected and to perish."[1]

Moreover, even if evil cannot be altogether avoided, it is no doubt true that not only whether the life we lead be good and useful, or evil and useless, but also whether it be happy or unhappy, is very much in our own power, and depends greatly on ourselves. "Time alone relieves the foolish from sorrow, but reason the wise,"[2] and no one was ever yet made utterly miserable excepting by himself. We are, if not the masters, at any rate almost the creators of ourselves.

With most of us it is not so much great sorrows, disease, or death, but rather the little "daily dyings" which cloud over the sunshine of life. Many of our troubles are insignificant in themselves, and might easily be avoided!

How happy home might generally be made but for foolish quarrels, or misunderstandings, as they are well named! It is our own fault if we are querulous or ill-humored; nor need we, though this is less easy, allow ourselves to be made unhappy by the querulousness or ill-humors of others.

Much of what we suffer we have brought on our-

[1] Epictetus. [2] *Ibid.*

selves, if not by actual fault, at least by ignorance or thoughtlessness. Too often we think only of the happiness of the moment, and sacrifice that of the life. Troubles comparatively seldom come to us, it is we who go to them. Many of us fritter our life away. La Bruyère says that "most men spend much of their lives in making the rest miserable;" or, as Goethe puts it:

> "Careworn man has, in all ages,
> Sown vanity to reap despair."

Not only do we suffer much in the anticipation of evil, as "Noah lived many years under the affliction of a flood, and Jerusalem was taken unto Jeremy before it was besieged," but we often distress ourselves greatly in the apprehension of misfortunes which after all never happen at all. We should do our best and wait calmly the result. We often hear of people breaking down from overwork, but in nine cases out of ten they are really suffering from worry or anxiety.

"Nos maux moraux," says Rousseau, "sont tous dans l'opinion, hors un seul, qui est le crime; et celui-la dépend de nous: nos maux physiques nous détruisent, ou se détruisent. Le temps, ou la mort, sont nos remèdes."

> "Our remedies oft in ourselves do lie,
> Which we ascribe to heaven."[1]

[1] Shakespeare.

This, however, applies to the grown up. With children of course it is different. It is customary, but I think it is a mistake, to speak of happy childhood. Children, however, are often over-anxious and acutely sensitive. Man ought to be man and master of his fate; but children are at the mercy of those around them. Mr. Rarey, the great horse-tamer, has told us that he has known an angry word raise the pulse of a horse ten beats in a minute. Think then how it must affect a child!

It is small blame to the young if they are over-anxious; but it is a danger to be striven against. "The terrors of the storm are chiefly felt in the parlor or the cabin."[1]

To save ourselves from imaginary, or at any rate problematical, evils, we often incur real suffering. "The man," said Epicurus, "who is not content with little is content with nothing." How often do we "labor for that which satisfieth not." More than we use is more than we need, and only a burden to the bearer.[2] We most of us give ourselves an immense amount of useless trouble; encumber ourselves, as it were, on the journey of life with a dead weight of unnecessary baggage; and as "a man maketh his train longer, he makes his wings shorter."[3] In that delightful fairy tale, *Alice through the Looking-Glass*, the "White Knight" is described as having loaded himself on starting for a journey with a variety of odds and

[1] Emerson.   [2] Seneca.   [3] Bacon.

ends, including a mousetrap, in case he was troubled by mice at night, and a beehive in case he came across a swarm of bees.

Hearne, in his *Journey to the Mouth of the Coppermine River*, tells us that a few days after starting on his expedition he met a party of Indians, who annexed a great deal of his property, and all Hearne says is, "The weight of our baggage being so much lightened, our next day's journey was much pleasanter." I ought, however, to add that the Indians broke up the philosophical instruments, which, no doubt, were rather an encumbrance.

When troubles do come, Marcus Aurelius wisely tells us to "remember on every occasion which leads thee to vexation to apply this principle, that this is not a misfortune, but that to bear it nobly is good fortune." Our own anger indeed does us more harm than the thing which makes us angry; and we suffer much more from the anger and vexation which we allow acts to rouse in us, than we do from the acts themselves at which we are angry and vexed. How much most people, for instance, allow themselves to be distracted and disturbed by quarrels and family disputes. Yet in nine cases out of ten one ought not to suffer from being found fault with. If the condemnation is just, it should be welcome as a warning; if it is undeserved, why should we allow it to distress us?

Moreover, if misfortunes happen we do but make them worse by grieving over them.

"I must die," again says Epictetus. "But

must I then die sorrowing? I must be put in chains. Must I then also lament? I must go into exile. Can I be prevented from going with cheerfulness and contentment? But I will put you in prison. Man, what are you saying? You may put my body in prison, but my mind not even Zeus himself can overpower."

If, indeed, we cannot be happy, the fault is generally in ourselves. Socrates lived under the Thirty Tyrants. Epictetus was a poor slave, and yet how much we owe him!

"How is it possible," he says, "that a man who has nothing, who is naked, houseless, without a hearth, squalid, without a slave, without a city, can pass a life that flows easily? See, God has sent a man to show you that it is possible. Look at me, who am without a city, without a house, without possessions, without a slave; I sleep on the ground; I have no wife, no children, no prætorium, but only the earth and heavens, and one poor clock. And what do I want? Am I not without sorrow? Am I not without fear? Am I not free? When did any of you see me failing in the object of my desire? or ever falling into that which I would avoid? Did I ever blame God or man? Did I ever accuse any man? Did any of you ever see me with a sorrowful countenance? And how do I meet with those whom you are afraid of and admire? Do not I treat them like slaves? Who, when he sees me, does not think that he sees his king and master?"

Think how much we have to be thankful for. Few of us appreciate the number of our everyday blessings; we look on them as trifles, and yet "trifles make perfection, and perfection is no trifle," as Michael Angelo said. We forget them because they are always with us; and yet for each of us, as Mr. Pater well observes, "these simple gifts, and others equally trivial, bread and wine, fruit and milk, might regain that poetic and, as it were, moral significance which surely belongs to all the means of our daily life, could we but break through the veil of our familiarity with things by no means vulgar in themselves."

"Let not," says Isaak Walton, "the blessings we receive daily from God make us not to value or not praise Him because they be common; let us not forget to praise Him for the innocent mirth and pleasure we have met with since we met together. What would a blind man give to see the pleasant rivers and meadows and flowers and fountains; and this and many other like blessings we enjoy daily."

Contentment, we have been told by Epicurus, consists not in great wealth, but in few wants. In this fortunate country, however, we may have many wants, and yet, if they are only reasonable, we may gratify them all.

Nature indeed provides without stint the main requisites of human happiness. "To watch the corn grow, or the blossoms set; to draw hard breath over plough-share or spade; to read, to think, to love, to pray," these, says Ruskin, "are the things that make men happy."

"I have fallen into the hands of thieves," says Jeremy Taylor; "what then? They have left me the sun and moon, fire and water, a loving wife and many friends to pity me, and some to relieve me, and I can still discourse; and, unless I list, they have not taken away my merry countenance and my cheerful spirit and a good conscience. . . . And he that hath so many causes of joy, and so great, is very much in love with sorrow and peevishness who loses all these pleasures, and chooses to sit down on his little handful of thorns."

"When a man has such things to think on, and sees the sun, the moon, and stars, and enjoys earth and sea, he is not solitary or even helpless."[1]

"Paradise indeed might," as Luther said, "apply to the whole world." What more is there we could ask for ourselves? "Every sort of beauty," says Mr. Greg,[2] "has been lavished on our allotted home; beauties to enrapture every sense, beauties to satisfy every taste; forms the noblest and the loveliest, colors the most gorgeous and the most delicate, odors the sweetest and subtlest, harmonies the most soothing and the most stirring: the sunny glories of the day; the pale Elysian grace of moonlight; the lake, the mountain, the primeval forest, and the boundless ocean; 'silent pinnacles of aged snow' in one hemisphere, the marvels of tropical luxuriance in another; the

[1] Epictetus.   [2] *The Enigmas of Life.*

serenity of sunsets; the sublimity of storms; everything is bestowed in boundless profusion on the scene of our existence; we can conceive or desire nothing more exquisite or perfect than what is round us every hour; and our perceptions are so framed as to be consciously alive to all. The provision made for our sensuous enjoyment is in overflowing abundance; so is that for the other elements of our complex nature. Who that has revelled in the opening ecstasies of a young Imagination, or the rich marvels of the world of Thought, does not confess that the Intelligence has been dowered at least with as profuse a beneficence as the Senses? Who that has truly tasted and fathomed human Love in its dawning and crowning joys has not thanked God for a felicity which indeed 'passeth understanding.' If we had set our fancy to picture a Creator occupied solely in devising delight for children whom he loved, we could not conceive one single element of bliss which is not here."

CHAPTER II.

THE HAPPINESS OF DUTY.

"I am always content with that which happens; for I think that what God chooses is better than what I choose."
EPICTETUS.

"O God, All conquering! this lower earth
Would be for men the blest abode of mirth
If they were strong in Thee
As other things of this world well are seen;
Oh then, far' other than they yet have been,
How happy would men be."
KING ALFRED'S ed. of Boethius's
Consolations of Philosophy.

WE ought not to picture Duty to ourselves, or to others, as a stern taskmistress. She is rather a kind and sympathetic mother, ever ready to shelter us from the cares and anxieties of this world, and to guide us in the paths of peace.

To shut oneself up from mankind is, in most cases, to lead a dull, as well as a selfish life. Our duty is to make ourselves useful, and thus life may be most interesting, and yet comparatively free from anxiety.

THE HAPPINESS OF DUTY. 21

But how can we fill our lives with *life*, energy, and interest, and yet keep care outside?

Many great men have made shipwreck in the attempt. "Anthony sought for happiness in love; Brutus in glory; Cæsar in dominion: the first found disgrace, the second disgust, the last ingratitude, and each destruction."[1] Riches, again, often bring danger, trouble, and temptation; they require care to keep, though they may give much happiness if wisely spent.

How then is this great object to be secured? What, says Marcus Aurelius, "What is that which is able to conduct a man? One thing and only one—philosophy. But this consists in keeping the dæmon[2] within a man free from violence and unharmed, superior to pains and pleasures, doing nothing without a purpose, yet not falsely and with hypocrisy, not feeling the need of another man's doing or not doing anything; and besides, accepting all that happens, and all that is allotted, as coming from thence, wherever it is, from whence he himself came; and, finally, waiting for death with a cheerful mind, as being nothing else than a dissolution of the elements of which every living being is compounded." I confess I do not feel the force of these last few words, which indeed scarcely seem requisite for his argument. The thought of death, however, certainly in-

[1] Colton, *Lacon, or Many Things in Few Words.*
[2] *I. e.* spirit.

fluences the conduct of life less than might have been expected.

Bacon truly points out that "there is no passion in the mind of man so weak, but it mates and masters the fear of death. . . . Revenge triumphs over death, love slights it, honor aspireth to it, grief flieth to it."

> "Think not I dread to see my spirit fly
> Through the dark gates of fell mortality;
> Death has no terrors when the life is true;
> 'Tis living ill that makes us fear to die." [1]

We need certainly have no such fear if we have done our best to make others happy; to promote "peace on earth and goodwill amongst men." Nothing, again, can do more to release us from the cares of this world, which consume so much of our time, and embitter so much of our life. When we have done our best, we should wait the result in peace; content, as Epictetus says, "with that which happens, for what God chooses is better than what I choose."

At any rate, if we have not effected all we wished, we shall have influenced ourselves. It may be true that one cannot do much. "You are not Hercules, and you are not able to purge away the wickedness of others; nor yet are you Theseus, able to drive away the evil things of Attica. But you may clear away your own. From yourself, from your own thoughts, cast away,

[1] Omar Khayyam.

instead of Procrustes and Sciron,[1] sadness, fear, desire, envy, malevolence, avarice, effeminacy, intemperance. But it is not possible to eject these things otherwise than by looking to God only, by fixing your affections on Him only, by being consecrated by his commands."[2]

People sometimes think how delightful it would be to be quite free. But a fish, as Ruskin says, is freer than a man, and as for a fly, it is "a black incarnation of freedom." A life of so-called pleasure and self-indulgence is not a life of real happiness or true freedom. Far from it, if we once begin to give way to ourselves, we fall under a most intolerable tyranny. Other temptations are in some respects like that of drink. At first, perhaps, it seems delightful, but there is bitterness at the bottom of the cup. Men drink to satisfy the desire created by previous indulgence. So it is in other things. Repetition soon becomes a craving, not a pleasure. Resistance grows more and more painful; yielding, which at first, perhaps, afforded some slight and temporary gratification, soon ceases to give pleasure, and even if for a time it procures relief, ere long becomes odious itself.

To resist is difficult, to give way is painful; until at length the wretched victim to himself, can only purchase, or thinks he can only purchase, temporary relief from intolerable craving and de-

---

[1] Two robbers destroyed by Theseus. [2] Epictetus.

pression, at the expense of far greater suffering in the future.

On the other hand, self-control, however difficult at first, becomes step by step easier and more delightful. We possess mysteriously a sort of dual nature, and there are few truer triumphs, or more delightful sensations, than to obtain thorough command of oneself.

How much pleasanter it is to ride a spirited horse, even perhaps though requiring some strength and skill, than to creep along upon a jaded hack. In the one case you feel under you the free, responsive spring of a living and willing force ; in the other you have to spur a dull and lifeless slave.

To rule oneself is in reality the greatest triumph. "He who is his own monarch," says Sir T. Browne, "contentedly sways the sceptre of himself, not envying the glory to crowned heads and Elohim of the earth ; " for those are really highest who are nearest to heaven, and those are lowest who are farthest from it.

True greatness has little, if anything, to do with rank or power. "Eurystheus being what he was," says Epictetus, "was not really king of Argos nor of Mycenæ, for he could not even rule himself; while Hercules purged lawlessness and introduced justice, though he was both naked and alone."

We are told that Cineas the philosopher once asked Pyrrhus what he would do when he had conquered Italy. "I will conquer Sicily." "And after Sicily?" "Then Africa." "And after you have conquered the world?" "I will take my ease and be merry." "Then," asked Cineas, "why can you not take your ease and be merry now?"

Moreover, as Sir Arthur Helps has wisely pointed out, "the enlarged view we have of the Universe must in some measure damp personal ambition. What is it to be king, sheikh, tetrarch, or emperor over a 'bit of a bit' of this little earth?" "All rising to great place," says Bacon, "is by a winding stair;" and "princes are like heavenly bodies, which have much veneration, but no rest."

Plato in the *Republic* mentions an old myth that after death every soul has to choose a lot in life for the existence in the next world; and he tells us that the wise Ulysses searched for a considerable time for the lot of a private man. He had some difficulty in finding it, as it was lying neglected in a corner, but when he had secured it he was delighted; the recollection of all he had gone through on earth, having disenchanted him of ambition.

Moreover, there is a great deal of drudgery in the lives of courts. Ceremonials may be important, but they take up much time and are terribly tedious.

A man then is his own best kingdom. "He that ruleth his speech," says Solomon, "is better than he that taketh a city." But self-control, this truest and greatest monarchy, rarely comes by inheritance. Every one of us must conquer himself; and we may do so, if we take conscience for our guide and general.

No one really fails who does his best. Seneca observes that "no one saith the three hundred Fabii were defeated, but that they were slain," and if you have done your best, you will, in the words of an old Norse ballad, have gained

"Success in thyself, which is best of all."

Being myself engaged in business, I was rather startled to find it laid down by no less an authority than Aristotle (almost as if it were a self-evident proposition) that commerce " is incompatible with that dignified life which it is our wish that our citizens should lead, and totally adverse to that generous elevation of mind with which it is our ambition to inspire them." I know not how far that may really have been the spirit and tendency of commerce among the ancient Greeks; but if so, I do not wonder that it was not more successful.

I may, indeed, quote Aristotle against himself, for he has elsewhere told us that "business should be chosen for the sake of leisure; and things necessary and useful for the sake of the beautiful in conduct."

It is not true that the ordinary duties of life in a country like ours—commerce, manufactures, agriculture,—the pursuits to which the vast majority are and must be devoted—are incompatible with the dignity or nobility of life. Whether a life is noble or ignoble depends, not on the calling which is adopted, but on the spirit in which it is followed. The humblest life may be noble, while that of the most powerful monarch or the greatest genius may be contemptible. Commerce, indeed, is not only compatible, but I would almost go further and say that it will be most successful, if carried on in happy union with noble aims and generous aspirations. What Ruskin says of art is, with due modification, true of life generally. It does not matter whether a man "paint the petal of a rose or the chasms of a precipice, so that love and admiration attend on him as he labors, and wait for ever on his work. It does not matter whether he toil for months on a few inches of his canvas, or cover a palace front with color in a day; so only that it be with a solemn purpose, that he have filled his heart with patience, or urged his hand to haste."

It is true that in a subsequent volume he refers to this passage, and adds, "But though all is good for study, and all is beautiful, some is better than the rest for the help and pleasure of others; and this it is our duty always to choose if we have opportunity," adding, however, "being quite happy with what is within our reach if we have not."

We read of and admire the heroes of old, but every one of us has to fight his own Marathon and Thermopylæ; every one meets the Sphinx sitting by the road he has to pass; to each of us, as to Hercules, is offered the choice of Vice or Virtue;

we may, like Paris, give the apple of life to Venus, or Juno, or Minerva.

There are many who seem to think that we have fallen on an age in the world when life is especially difficult and anxious, when there is less leisure than of yore, and the struggle for existence is keener than ever.

On the other hand, we must remember how much we have gained in security? It may be an age of hard work, but when this is not carried to an extreme, it is by no means an evil. If we have less leisure, one reason is because life is so full of interest. Cheerfulness is the daughter of employment, and on the whole I believe there never was a time when modest merit and patient industry were more sure of reward.

We must not, indeed, be discouraged if success be slow in coming, nor puffed up if it comes quickly. We often complain of the nature of things when the fault is all in ourselves. Seneca, in one of his letters, mentions that his wife's maid, Harpaste, had nearly lost her eyesight, but " she knoweth not she is blind, she saith the house is dark. This that seemeth ridiculous unto us in her, happeneth unto us all. No man understandeth that he is covetous, or avaricious. He saith, I am not ambitious, but no man can otherwise live in Rome; I am not sumptuous, but the city requireth great expense."

Newman, in perhaps the most beautiful of his hymns, " Lead, kindly light," says :

"Keep thou my feet, I do not ask to see
The distant scene; one step enough for me."

But we must be sure that we are really following some trustworthy guide, and not out of mere laziness allowing ourselves to drift. We have a guide within us which will generally lead us straight enough.

Religion, no doubt, is full of difficulties, but if we are often puzzled what to think, we need seldom be in doubt what to do.

"To say well is good, but to do well is better;
Do well is the spirit, and say well the letter;
If do well and say well were fitted in one frame,
All were won, all were done, and got were all the gain."

Cleanthes, who appears to have well merited the statue erected to him at Assos, says:

"Lead me, O Zeus, and thou, O Destiny,
The way that I am bid by you to go:
To follow I am ready. If I choose not,
I make myself a wretch;—and still must follow."

If we are ever in doubt what to do, it is a good rule to ask ourselves what we shall wish on the morrow that we had done.

Moreover, the result in the long run will depend not so much on some single resolution, or on our action in a special case, but rather on the preparation of daily life. Battles are often won before they are fought. To control our passions we must govern our habits, and keep watch over ourselves in the small details of everyday life.

The importance of small things has been pointed out by philosophers over and over again from Æsop downward. "Great without small makes a bad wall," says a quaint Greek proverb, which seems to go back to cyclopean times. In an old Hindoo story Ammi says to his son, "Bring me a fruit of that tree and break it open. What is there?" The son said, "Some small seeds." "Break one of them and what do you see?" "Nothing, my lord." "My child," said Ammi, "where you see nothing there dwells a mighty tree." It may almost be questioned whether anything can be truly called small.

> "There is no great and no small
> To the soul that maketh all;
> And where it cometh all things are,
> And it cometh everywhere." [1]

We should therefore watch ourselves in small things. If "you wish not to be of an angry temper, do not feed the habit: throw nothing on it which will increase it: at first keep quiet, and count the days on which you have not been angry. I used to be in passion every day; now every second day; then every third; then every fourth. But if you have intermitted thirty days, make a sacrifice to God. For the habit at first begins to

[1] Emerson.

be weakened, and then is completely destroyed. When you can say, 'I have not been vexed to-day, nor the day before, nor yet on any succeeding day during two or three months; but I took care when some exciting things happened,' be assured that you are in a good way."[1]

Emerson closes his *Conduct of Life* with a striking allegory. The young Mortal enters the Hall of the Firmament. The Gods are sitting there, and he is alone with them. They pour on him gifts and blessings, and beckon him to their thrones. But between him and them suddenly appear snow-storms of illusions. He imagines himself in a vast crowd, whose behests he fancies he must obey. The mad crowd drives hither and thither, and sways this way and that. What is he that he should resist? He lets himself be carried about. How can he think or act for himself? But the clouds lift, and there are the Gods still sitting on their thrones; they alone with him alone.

"The great man," he elsewhere says, "is he who in the midst of the crowd keeps with perfect sweetness the serenity of solitude."

We may all, if we will, secure peace of mind for ourselves.

"Men seek retreats," says Marcus Aurelius, "houses in the country, seashores, and mountains; and thou too art wont to desire such things very much. But this is altogether a mark of the most

[1] Epictetus.

common sort of men; for it is in thy power whenever thou shalt choose, to retire into thyself. For nowhere either with more quiet or more freedom from trouble does a man retire, than into his own soul, particularly when he has within him such thoughts that by looking into them he is immediately in perfect tranquillity."

Happy indeed is he who has such a sanctuary in his own soul. "He who is virtuous is wise; and he who is wise is good; and he who is good is happy."[1]

But we cannot expect to be happy if we do not lead pure and useful lives. To be good company for ourselves we must store our minds well; fill them with pure and peaceful thoughts; with pleasant memories of the past, and reasonable hopes for the future. We must, as far as may be, protect ourselves from self-reproach, from care, and from anxiety. We shall make our lives pure and peaceful, by resisting evil, by placing restraint upon our appetites, and perhaps even more by strengthening and developing our tendencies to good. We must be careful, then, on what we allow our minds to dwell. The soul is dyed by its thoughts; we cannot keep our minds pure if we allow them to be sullied by detailed accounts of crime and sin. Peace of mind, as Ruskin beautifully observes, "must come in its own time, as the waters settle themselves into clearness as well as quietness; you can no more filter your mind into purity than you

[1] King Alfred's *Boethius*.

can compress it into calmness ; you must keep it pure if you would have it pure, and throw no stones into it if you would have it quiet."

The penalty of injustice, said Socrates, is not death or stripes, but the fatal necessity of becoming more and more unjust. Few men have led a wiser or more virtuous life than Socrates himself, of whom Xenophon gives us the following description :—" To me, being such as I have described him, so pious that he did nothing without the sanction of the gods ; so just, that he wronged no man even in the most trifling affair, but was of service in the most important matters to those who enjoyed his society ; so temperate that he never preferred pleasure to virtue ; so wise, that he never erred in distinguishing better from worse ; needing no counsel from others, but being sufficient in himself to discriminate between them ; so able to explain and settle such questions by argument ; and so capable of discerning the character of others, of confuting those who were in error, and of exhorting them to virtue and honor, he seemed to be such as the best and happiest of men would be. But if any one disapproves of my opinion let him compare the conduct of others with that of Socrates, and determine accordingly."

Marcus Aurelius again has drawn for us a most instructive lesson in his character of Antoninus :— " Remember his constancy in every act which was conformable to reason, his evenness in all things, his piety, the serenity of his countenance, his sweetness, his disregard of empty fame, and his efforts to understand things; how he would never let anything pass without having first carefully examined it and clearly understood it; how he bore with those who blamed him unjustly without blaming them in return; how he did nothing in a hurry; how he listened not to calumnies, and how exact an examiner of manners and actions he was; not given to reproach people, nor timid, nor suspicious, nor a sophist; with how little he was satisfied, such as lodging, bed, dress, food, servants; how laborious and patient; how sparing he was in his diet; his firmness and uniformity in his friendships; how he tolerated freedom of speech in those who opposed his opinions; the pleasure that he had when any man showed him anything better; and how pious he was without superstition. Imitate all this that thou mayest have as good a conscience, when thy last hour comes, as he had."

Such peace of mind is indeed an inestimable boon, a rich reward of duty fulfilled. Well then does Epictetus ask, "Is there no reward? Do you seek a reward greater than that of doing what is good and just? At Olympia you wish for nothing more, but it seems to you enough to be crowned at the games. Does it then seem to you so small and worthless a thing to be good and happy?"

In Bernard of Morlaix's beautiful lines—

> "Pax erit illa fidelibus, illa beata
> Irrevocabilis, Invariabilis, Intemerata.

Pax sine crimine, pax sine turbine, pax sine rixâ,
Meta Laboribus, inque tumultibus anchora fixa;
Pax erit omnibus unica. Sed quibus? Immaculatis
Pectore mitibus, ordine stantibus, ore sacratis."

What greater reward can we have than this; than the " peace which passeth all understanding," " which cannot be gotten for gold, neither shall silver be weighed for the price thereof." [1]

[1] Job.

CHAPTER III.

A SONG OF BOOKS.

> "Oh for a booke and a shadie nooke,
>   Eyther in doore or out;
> With the grene leaves whispering overhead
>   Or the streete cryes all about.
> Where I maie reade all at my ease,
>   Both of the newe and old;
> For a jollie goode booke whereon to looke,
>   Is better to me than golde."
> OLD ENGLISH SONG.

OF all the privileges we enjoy in this nineteenth century there is none, perhaps, for which we ought to be more thankful than for the easier access to books.

The debt we owe to books was well expressed by Richard de Bury, Bishop of Durham, author of *Philobiblon*, written as long ago as 1344, published in 1473, and the earliest English treatise on the delights of literature:—"These," he says, "are the masters who instruct us without rods and ferules, without hard words and anger, without clothes or money. If you approach them, they are not asleep; if investigating you interrogate them, they conceal nothing; if you mistake them, they never grumble; if you are ignorant, they cannot laugh at you. The library, therefore, of wisdom is more precious than all riches, and nothing that can be wished for is worthy to be compared with it. Whosoever therefore acknowledges himself to be a zealous follower of truth, of happiness, of wisdom, of science, or even of the faith, must of necessity make himself a lover of books." But if the debt were great then, how much more now.

This feeling that books are real friends is constantly present to all who love reading. "I have friends," said Petrarch, "whose society is extremely agreeable to me; they are of all ages, and of every country. They have distinguished themselves both in the cabinet and in the field, and obtained high honors for their knowledge of the sciences. It is easy to gain access to them, for they are always at my service, and I admit them to my company, and dismiss them from it, whenever I please. They are never troublesome, but immediately answer every question I ask them. Some relate to me the events of past ages, while others reveal to me the secrets of Nature. Some teach me how to live, and others how to die. Some, by their vivacity, drive away my cares and exhilarate my spirits; while others give fortitude to my mind, and teach me the important lesson how to restrain my desires, and to depend wholly on myself. They open to me, in short, the various avenues of all the arts and sciences, and upon their information I may safely rely in all emergencies. In return for all their services, they only ask me to accommodate them with a convenient chamber in some corner of my humble habitation, where they may repose in peace; for these friends are more delighted by the tranquillity of retirement than with the tumults of society."

"He that loveth a book," says Isaac Barrow, "will never want a faithful friend, a wholesome counsellor, a cheerful companion, an effectual comforter. By study, by reading, by thinking, one may innocently divert and pleasantly entertain himself, as in all weathers, so in all fortunes."

Southey took a rather more melancholy view:

> "My days among the dead are pass'd,
> Around me I behold,
> Where'er these casual eyes are cast,
> The mighty minds of old.
> My never-failing friends are they,
> With whom I converse day by day."

Imagine, in the words of Aikin, "that we had it in our power to call up the shades of the greatest and wisest men that ever existed, and oblige them to converse with us on the most interesting topics—what an inestimable privilege should we think it!—how superior to all common enjoyments! But in a well-furnished library we, in fact, possess this power. We can question Xenophon and Cæsar on their campaigns, make Demosthenes and Cicero plead before us, join in the audiences of Socrates and Plato, and receive demonstrations from Euclid and Newton. In books we have the choicest thoughts of the ablest men in their best dress."

"Books," says Jeremy Collier, "are a guide in youth and an entertainment for age. They support us under solitude, and keep us from being a burthen to ourselves. They help us to forget the crossness of men and things; compose our cares and our passions; and lay our disappointments asleep. When we are weary of the living, we may repair to the dead, who have nothing of peevishness, pride, or design in their conversation."

Sir John Herschel tells an amusing anecdote illustrating the pleasure derived from a book, not assuredly of the first order. In a certain village the blacksmith having got hold of Richardson's novel, *Pamela, or Virtue Rewarded*, used to sit on his anvil in the long summer evenings and read it aloud to a large and attentive audience. It is by no means a short book, but they fairly listened to it all. At length, when the happy turn of fortune arrived, which brings the hero and heroine together, and sets them living long and happily together according to the most approved rules, the congregation were so delighted as to raise a great shout, and procuring the church keys, actually set the parish bells a-ringing.

"The lover of reading," says Leigh Hunt, "will derive agreeable terror from *Sir Bertram* and the *Haunted Chamber;* will assent with delighted reason to every sentence in *Mrs. Bar-*

bauld's Essay; will feel himself wandering into solitudes with *Gray;* shake honest hands with *Sir Roger de Coverley;* be ready to embrace *Parson Adams,* and to chuck *Pounce* out of the window instead of the hat; will travel with *Marco Polo* and *Mungo Park;* stay at home with *Thomson;* retire with *Cowley;* be industrious with *Hutton;* sympathizing with *Gay* and *Mrs. Inchbald;* laughing with (and at) *Buncle;* melancholy, and forlorn, and self-restored with the shipwrecked mariner of *De Foe.*"

Carlyle has wisely said that a collection of books is a real university.

The importance of books has been appreciated in many quarters where we might least expect it. Among the hardy Norsemen runes were supposed to be endowed with miraculous power. There is an Arabic proverb, that "a wise man's day is worth a fool's life," and another—though it reflects perhaps rather the spirit of the Califs than of the Sultans,—that "the ink of science is more precious than the blood of the martyrs."

Confucius is said to have described himself as a man who "in his eager pursuit of knowledge forgot his food, who in the joy of its attainment forgot his sorrows, and did not even perceive that old age was coming on."

Yet, if this could be said by the Arabs and the Chinese, what language can be strong enough to express the gratitude we ought to feel for the advantages we enjoy! We do not appreciate, I think, our good fortune in belonging to the nineteenth century. Sometimes, indeed, one may even be inclined to wish that one had not lived quite so soon, and to long for a glimpse of the books, even the school-books, of one hundred years hence. A hundred years ago not only were books extremely expensive and cumbrous, but many of the most delightful were still uncreated—such as the works of Scott, Thackeray, Dickens, Bulwer Lytton, and Trollope, not to mention living authors. How much more interesting science has become especially, if I were to mention only one name, through the genius of Darwin! Renan has characterized this as a most amusing century; I should rather have described it as most interesting : presenting us as it does with an endless vista of absorbing problems; with infinite opportunities ; with more interest and less danger than surrounded our less fortunate ancestors.

Cicero described a room without books, as a body without a soul. But it is by no means necessary to be a philosopher to love reading.

Reading, indeed, is by no means necessarily study. Far from it. "I put," says Mr. Frederic Harrison, in his excellent article on the "Choice of Books," "I put the poetic and emotional side of literature as the most needed for daily use."

In the prologue to the *Legende of Goode Women*, Chaucer says:

> "And as for me, though that I konne but lyte,
> On bokes for to rede I me delyte,
> And to him give I feyth and ful credence,
> And in myn herte have him in reverence,
> So hertely, that ther is game noon,
> That fro my bokes maketh me to goon,
> But yt be seldome on the holy day,
> Save, certynly, when that the monthe of May
> Is comen, and that I here the foules synge,
> And that the floures gynnen for to sprynge,
> Farwel my boke and my devocion."

But I doubt whether, if he had enjoyed our advantages, he could have been so certain of tearing himself away, even in the month of May.

Macaulay, who had all that wealth and fame, rank and talents could give, yet, we are told, derived his greatest happiness from books. Sir G. Trevelyan, in his charming biography, says that—"of the feelings which Macaulay entertained toward the great minds of bygone ages it is not for any one except himself to speak. He has told us how his debt to them was incalculable; how they guided him to truth; how they filled his mind with noble and graceful images; how they stood by him in all vicissitudes—comforters in sorrow, nurses in sickness, companions in solitude, the old friends who are never seen with new faces; who are the same in wealth and in poverty, in glory and in obscurity. Great as were the honors and possessions which Macaulay acquired by his pen, all who knew him were well aware that the titles and rewards which he gained by his own works were as nothing in the balance compared with the pleasure he derived from the works of others."

There was no society in London so agreeable that Macaulay would have preferred it at breakfast or at dinner "to the company of Sterne or Fielding, Horace Walpole or Boswell." The love of reading which Gibbon declared he would not exchange for all the treasures of India was, in fact, with Macaulay "a main element of happiness in one of the happiest lives that it has ever fallen to the lot of the biographer to record."

"History," says Fuller, "maketh a young man to be old without either wrinkles or gray hair, privileging him with the experience of age without either the infirmities or the inconveniences thereof."

So delightful indeed are books that we must be careful not to forget other duties for them; in cultivating the mind we must not neglect the body.

To the lover of literature or science, exercise often presents itself as an irksome duty, and many a one has felt like "the fair pupil of Ascham (Lady Jane Gray), who, while the horns were sounding and dogs in full cry, sat in the lonely oriel, with eyes riveted to that immortal page which tells how meekly and bravely (Socrates) the first martyr of intellectual liberty took the cup from his weeping jailer." [1]

[1] Macaulay.

Still, as the late Lord Derby justly observed,[1] those who do not find time for exercise will have to find time for illness.

Books, again, are now so cheap as to be within the reach of almost every one. This was not always so. It is quite a recent blessing. Mr. Ireland, to whose charming little *Book Lover's Enchiridion*, in common with every lover of reading, I am greatly indebted, tells us that when a boy he was so delighted with White's *Natural History of Selborne*, that in order to possess a copy of his own he actually copied out the whole work.

Mary Lamb gives a pathetic description of a studious boy lingering at a bookstall:

> "I saw a boy with eager eye
> Open a book upon a stall,
> And read, as he'd devour it all;
> Which, when the stall man did espy,
> Soon to the boy I heard him call,
> 'You, sir, you never buy a book,
> Therefore in one you shall not look.'
> The boy passed slowly on, and with a sigh
> He wished he never had been taught to read,
> Then of the old churl's books he should have had no
>   need."

Such snatches of literature have indeed, special and peculiar charm. This is, I believe, partly due to the very fact of their being brief. Many readers miss much of the pleasure of reading by forcing themselves to dwell too long continuously

[1] Address, Liverpool College, 1873.

on one subject. In a long railway journey, for instance, many persons take only a single book. The consequence is that, unless it is a story, after half an hour or an hour they are quite tired of it. Whereas, if they had two, or still better three books, on different subjects, and one of them of an amusing character, they would probably find that, by changing as soon as they felt at all weary, they would come back again and again to each with renewed zest, and hour after hour would pass pleasantly away. Every one, of course, must judge for himself, but such at least is my experience.

I quite agree, therefore, with Lord Iddesleigh as to the charm of desultory reading, but the wider the field the more important that we should benefit by the very best books in each class. Not that we need confine ourselves to them, but that we should commence with them, and they will certainly lead us on to others. There are of course some books which we must read, mark, learn, and inwardly digest. But these are exceptions. As regards by far the larger number, it is probably better to read them quickly, dwelling only on the best and most important passages. In this way, no doubt, we shall lose much, but we gain more by ranging over a wider field. We may, in fact, I think, apply to reading Lord Brougham's wise dictum as regards education, and say that it is well to read everything of something, and something of everything. In this way only we can ascertain the bent of our own tastes, for it is a general, though not of course an invariable, rule, that we profit little by books which we do not enjoy.

Every one, however, may suit himself. The variety is endless.

Not only does a library contain "infinite riches in a little room,"[1] but we may sit at home and yet be in all quarters of the earth. We may travel round the world with Captain Cook or Darwin, with Kingsley or Ruskin, who will show us much more perhaps than ever we should see for ourselves. The world itself has no limits for us; Humboldt and Herschel will carry us far away to the mysterious nebulæ, beyond the sun and even the stars: time has no more bounds than space; history stretches out behind us, and geology will carry us back for millions of years before the creation of man, even to the origin of the material Universe itself. Nor are we limited to one plane of thought. Aristotle and Plato will transport us into a sphere none the less delightful because we cannot appreciate it without some training.

Comfort and consolation, refreshment and happiness, may indeed be found in his library by any one " who shall bring the golden key that unlocks its silent door."[2] A library is true fairyland, a very palace of delight, a haven of repose from the storms and troubles of the world. Rich and poor can enjoy it equally, for here, at least, wealth gives no advantage. We may make a library, if we do but rightly use it, a true paradise on earth, a gar-

---

[1] Marlowe. [2] Matthews.

den of Eden without its one drawback; for all is open to us, including, and especially, the fruit of the Tree of Knowledge, for which we are told that our first mother sacrificed all the Pleasures of Paradise. Here we may read the most important histories, the most exciting volumes of travels and adventures, the most interesting stories, the most beautiful poems; we may meet the most eminent statesmen, poets, and philosophers, benefit by the ideas of the greatest thinkers, and enjoy the grandest creations of human genius.

CHAPTER IV.

THE CHOICE OF BOOKS.

> " All round the room my silent servants wait
> My friends in every season, bright and dim,
> Angels and Seraphim
> Come down and murmur to me, sweet and low,
> And spirits of the skies all come and go
> Early and Late." PROCTOR.

AND yet too often they wait in vain. One reason for this is, I think, that people are overwhelmed by the crowd of books offered to them.

In old days books were rare and dear. Now on the contrary, it may be said with greater truth 'than ever that

> " Words are things, and a small drop of ink,
> Falling like dew upon a thought, produces
> That which makes thousands, perhaps millions, think."

Our ancestors had a difficulty in procuring them. Our difficulty now is what to select. We must be careful what we read, and not, like the sailors of

Ulysses, take bags of wind for sacks of treasure—not only lest we should even now fall into the error of the Greeks, and suppose that language and definitions can be instruments of investigation as well as of thought, but lest, as too often happens, we should waste time over trash. There are many books to which one may apply, in the sarcastic sense, the ambiguous remark said to have been made to an unfortunate author, "I will lose no time in reading your book."

There are, indeed, books and books, and there are books which, as Lamb said, are not books at all. It is wonderful how much innocent happiness we thoughtlessly throw away. An Eastern proverb says that calamities sent by heaven may be avoided, but from those we bring on ourselves there is no escape.

Many, I believe, are deterred from attempting what are called stiff books for fear they should not understand them; but there are few who need complain of the narrowness of their minds, if only they would do their best with them.

In reading, however, it is most important to select subjects in which one is interested. I remember years ago consulting Mr. Darwin as to the selection of a course of study. He asked me what interested me most, and advised me to choose that subject. This, indeed, applies to the work of life generally.

I am sometimes disposed to think that the readers of the next generation will be, not our lawyers and doctors, shopkeepers and manufacturers, but the laborers and mechanics. Does not this seem natural? The former work mainly with their head; when their daily duties are over the brain is often exhausted, and of their leisure time much must be devoted to air and exercise. The laborer and mechanic, on the contrary, besides working often for much shorter hours, have in their work-time taken sufficient bodily exercise, and could therefore give any leisure they might have to reading and study. They have not done so as yet, it is true; but this has been for obvious reasons. Now, however, in the first place, they receive an excellent education in elementary schools, and in the second have more easy access to the best books.

Ruskin has observed that he does not wonder at what men suffer, but he often wonders at what they lose. We suffer much, no doubt, from the faults of others, but we lose much more by our own ignorance.

"If," says Sir John Herschel, "I were to pray for a taste which should stand me in stead under every variety of circumstances, and be a source of happiness and cheerfulness to me through life, and a shield against its ills, however things might go amiss and the world frown upon me, it would be a taste for reading. I speak of it of course only as a worldly advantage, and not in the slightest degree as superseding or derogating from the higher office and surer and stronger panoply of religious principles—but as a taste, and instrument, and a mode of pleasurable gratification. Give a man this taste, and the means of gratifying it, and you can hardly fail of making a happy man, unless, indeed, you put into his hands a most perverse selection of books."

It is one thing to own a library; it is quite another to use it wisely. I have often been astonished how little care people devote to the selection of what they read. Books, we know, are almost innumerable; our hours for reading are, alas! very few. And yet many people read almost by hazard. They will take any book they chance to find in a room at a friend's house; they will buy a novel at a railway-stall if it has an attractive title; indeed, I believe in some cases even the binding affects their choice. The selection is, no doubt, far from easy. I have often wished some one would recommend a list of a hundred good books. If we had such lists drawn up by a few good guides they would be most useful. I have indeed sometimes heard it said that in reading every one must choose for himself, but this reminds me of the recommendation not to go into the water till you can swim.

In the absence of such lists I have picked out the books most frequently mentioned with approval by those who have referred directly or indirectly to the pleasure of reading, and have ventured to include some which, though less frequently mentioned, are especial favorites of my own. Every one who looks at the list will wish to suggest other books, as indeed I should myself, but in that case the number would soon run up.[1]

I have abstained, for obvious reasons, from mentioning works by living authors, though from many of them—Tennyson, Ruskin, and others—I have myself derived the keenest enjoyment; and I have omitted works on science, with one or two exceptions, because the subject is so progressive.

I feel that the attempt is over bold, and I must beg for indulgence, while hoping for criticism; indeed one object which I have had in view is to stimulate others more competent far than I am to give us the advantage of their opinions.

Moreover, I must repeat that I suggest these works rather as those which, as far as I have seen, have been most frequently recommended, than as suggestions of my own, though I have slipped in a few of my own special favorites.

In any such selection much weight should, I think, be attached to the general verdict of mankind. There is a "struggle for existence" and a "survival of the fittest" among books, as well as among animals and plants. As Alonzo of Aragon said, "Age is a recommendation in four things—old wood to burn, old wine to drink, old friends to trust, and old books to read." Still, this can-

---

[1] Several longer lists have been given; for instance, by Comte, *Catechism of Positive Philosophy;* Pycroft, *Course of English Reading;* Baldwin, *The Book Lover;* Perkins, *The Best Reading;* and by Mr. Ireland, *Books for General Readers.*

not be accepted without important qualifications. The most recent books of history and science contain or ought to contain, the most accurate information and the most trustworthy conclusions. Moreover, while the books of other races and times have an interest from their very distance, it must be admitted that many will still more enjoy, and feel more at home with, those of our own century and people.

Yet the oldest books of the world are remarkable and interesting on account of their very age; and the works which have influenced the opinions, or charmed the leisure hours, of millions of men in distant times and far-away regions are well worth reading on that very account, even if to us they seem scarcely to deserve their reputation. It is true that to many, such works are accessible only in translations; but translations, though they can never perhaps do justice to the original, may yet be admirable in themselves. The Bible itself, which must stand first in the list, is a conclusive case.

At the head of all non-Christian moralists, I must place the *Enchiridion* of Epictetus, certainly one of the noblest books in the whole of literature; it has, moreover, been admirably translated. With Epictetus,[1] I think must come Marcus Aurelius. The *Analects* of Confucius will, I believe, prove disappointing to most English readers, but the ef-

---

[1] It is much to be desired that some one would publish a selection from the works of Seneca.

fect it has produced on the most numerous race of men constitutes in itself a peculiar interest. The *Ethics* of Aristotle, perhaps, appear to some disadvantage from the very fact that they have so profoundly influenced our views of morality. The *Koran*, like the *Analects* of Confucius, will to most of us derive its principal interest from the effect it has exercised, and still exercises, on so many millions of our fellow-men. I doubt whether in any other respect it will seem to repay perusal, and to most persons probably certain extracts, not too numerous, would appear sufficient.

The writings of the Apostolic Fathers have been collected in one volume by Wake. It is but a small one, and though I must humbly confess that I was disappointed, they are perhaps all the more curious from the contrast they afford to those of the Apostles themselves. Of the later Fathers I have included only the *Confessions* of St. Augustine, which Dr. Pusey selected for the commencement of the *Library of the Fathers*, and which, as he observes, has "been translated again and again into almost every European language, and in all loved;" though Luther was of opinion that St. Augustine "wrote nothing to the purpose concerning faith." But then Luther was no great admirer of the Father. St. Jerome, he says, "writes, alas! very coldly;" Chrysostom "digresses from the chief points;" St. Jerome is "very poor;" and in fact, he says, "the more I read the books of the Fathers the more I find myself offended;" while

Renan, in his interesting autobiography, compared theology to a Gothic Cathedral, "elle a la grandeur, les vides immenses, et le peu de solidité."

Among other devotional works most frequently recommended are Thomas à Kempis' *Imitation of Christ*, Pascal's *Pensées*, Spinoza's *Tractatus Theologico-Politicus*, Butler's *Analogy of Religion*, Jeremy Taylor's *Holy Living and Dying*, Bunyan's *Pilgrim's Progress*, and last, not least, Keble's beautiful *Christian Year*.

Aristotle and Plato again stand at the head of another class. The *Politics* of Aristotle, and Plato's *Dialogues*, if not the whole, at any rate the *Phædo*, the *Apology*, and the *Republic*, will be of course read by all who wish to know anything of the history of human thought, though I am heretical enough to doubt whether the latter repays the minute and laborious study often devoted to it.

Aristotle being the father, if not the creator, of the modern scientific method, it has followed naturally—indeed, almost inevitably—that his principles have become part of our very intellectual being, so that they seem now almost self-evident, while his actual observations, though very remarkable—as, for instance, when he observes that bees on one journey confine themselves to one kind of flower—still have been in many cas s superseded by others, carried on under more favo - able conditions. We must not be ungrateful to the great master, because his lessons have taught us how to advance.

Plato, on the other hand, I say so with all respect, seems to me in some cases to play on words: his arguments are very able, very philosophical, often very noble; but not always conclusive; in a language differently constructed they might sometimes tell in exactly the opposite sense. If this method has proved less fruitful, if in metaphysics we have made but little advance, that very fact in one point of view leaves the *Dialogues* of Socrates as instructive now as ever they were; while the problems with which they deal will always rouse our interest, as the calm and lofty spirit which inspires them must command our admiration. Of the *Apology* and the *Phædo* especially it would be impossible to speak too gratefully.

I would also mention Demosthenes' *De Coronâ*, which Lord Brougham pronounced the greatest oration of the greatest of orators; Lucretius, Plutarch's Lives, Horace, and at least the *De Officiis*, *De Amicitiâ*, and *De Senectute* of Cicero.

The great epics of the world have always constituted one of the most popular branches of literature. Yet how few, comparatively, ever read Homer or Virgil after leaving school.

The *Nibelungenlied*, our great Anglo-Saxon epic, is perhaps too much neglected, no doubt on account of its painful character. Brunhild and Kriemhild, indeed, are far from perfect, but we meet with few such "live" women in Greek or Roman literature. Nor must I omit to mention Sir T. Malory's *Morte d'Arthur*, though I confess

I do so mainly in deference to the judgment of others.

Among the Greek tragedians I include Æschylus, if not all his works, at any rate *Prometheus*, perhaps the sublimest poem in Greek literature, and the *Trilogy* (Mr. Symonds in his *Greek Poets* speaks of the "unrivalled majesty" of the *Agamemnon*, and Mark Pattison considered it "the grandest work of creative genius in the whole range of literature"); or, as Sir M. E. Grant Duff recommends, the *Persæ;* Sophocles (*Œdipus Tyrannus*), Euripides (*Medea*), and Aristophanes (*The Knights* and *Clouds*); unfortunately, as Schlegel says, probably even the greatest scholar does not understand half his jokes; and I think most modern readers will prefer our modern poets.

I should like, moreover, to say a word for Eastern poetry, such as portions of the *Maha Bharata* and *Ramayana* (too long probably to be read through, but of which Talboys Wheeler has given a most interesting epitome in the first two volumes of his *History of India*); the *Shah-nameh*, the work of the great Persian poet Firdusi; Kalidasa's *Sakuntala*, and the Sheking, the classical collection of ancient Chinese odes. Many I know, will think I ought to have included Omar Khayyam.

In history we are beginning to feel that the vices and vicissitudes of kings and queens, the dates of battles and wars, are far less important than the development of human thought, the progress of art, of science, and of law, and the subject is on that very account even more interesting than ever. I will, however, only mention, and that rather from a literary than a historical point of view, Herodotus, Xenophon (the *Anabasis*), Thucydides, and Tacitus (*Germania*); and of modern historians, Gibbon's *Decline and Fall* ("the splendid bridge from the old world to the new"), Hume's *History of England*, Carlyle's *French Revolution*, Grote's *History of Greece*, and Green's *Short History of the English People*.

Science is so rapidly progressive that, though to many minds it is the most fruitful and interesting subject of all, I cannot here rest on that agreement which, rather than my own opinion, I take as the basis of my list. I will therefore only mention Bacon's *Novum Organum*, Mill's *Logic*, and Darwin's *Origin of Species ;* in Political Economy, which some of our rulers do not now sufficiently value, Mill, and parts of Smith's *Wealth of Nations*, for probably those who do not intend to make a special study of political economy would scarcely read the whole.

Among voyages and travels, perhaps those most frequently suggested are Cook's *Voyages*, Humboldt's *Travels*, and Darwin's *Naturalist's Journal ;* though I confess I should like to have added many more.

Mr. Bright not long ago specially recommended the less known American poets, but he probably assumed that every one would have read Shakespeare, Milton (*Paradise Lost, Lycidas, Comus* and minor poems), Chaucer, Dante, Spencer, Dryden, Scott, Wordsworth, Pope, Byron, and others, before embarking on more doubtful adventures.

Among other books most frequently recommended are Goldsmith's *Vicar of Wakefield*, Swift's *Gulliver's Travels*, Defoe's *Robinson Crusoe, The Arabian Nights, Don Quixote*, Boswell's *Life of Johnson*, White's *Natural History of Selborne*, Burke's Select Works (Payne), the Essays of Bacon, Addison, Hume, Montaigne, Macaulay, and Emerson, Carlyle's *Past and Present*, Smiles' *Self-Help*, and Goethe's *Faust* and *Autobiography*.

Nor can one go wrong in recommending Berkeley's *Human Knowledge*, Descartes' *Discours sur la Méthode*, Locke's *Conduct of the Understanding*, Lewes' *History of Philosophy;* while, in order to keep within the number one hundred, I can only mention Moliére and Sheridan among dramatists. Macaulay considered Marivaux's *La Vie de Marianne* the best novel in any language, but my number is so nearly complete that I must content myself with English: and will suggest Thackeray (*Vanity Fair* and *Pendennis*), Dickens (*Pickwick* and *David Copperfield*), G. Eliot (*Adam Bede* or *The Mill on the Floss*), Kingsley (*Westward Ho!*), Lytton (*Last Days of Pompeii*), and last, not least, those of Scott, which indeed constitute a library in themselves, but which

I must ask, in return for my trouble, to be allowed, as a special favor, to count as one.

To any lover of books the very mention of these names brings back a crowd of delicious memories, grateful recollections of peaceful home hours, after the labors and anxieties of the day. How thankful we ought to be for these inestimable blessings, for this numberless host of friends who never weary, betray, or forsake us!

LIST OF 100 BOOKS.

Works by Living Authors are omitted.

The Bible
The Meditations of Marcus Aurelius
Epictetus
Aristotle's Ethics
Analects of Confucius
St. Hilaire's " Le Bouddha et sa religion "
Wake's Apostolic Fathers
Thos. à Kempis' Imitation of Christ
Confessions of St. Augustine (Dr. Pusey)
The Koran (portions of)
Spinoza's Tractatus Theologico-Politicus
Comte's Catechism of Positive Philosophy
Pascal's Pensées
Butler's Analogy of Religion
Taylor's Holy Living and Dying
Bunyan's Pilgrim's Progress
Keble's Christian Year

Plato's Dialogues; at any rate, the Apology, Crito, and Phædo

Xenophon's Memorabilia
Aristotle's Politics
Demosthenes' De Coronâ
Cicero's De Officiis, De Amicitiâ, and De Senectute
Plutarch's Lives
Berkeley's Human Knowledge
Descartes' Discours sur la Méthode
Locke's On the Conduct of the Understanding

Homer
Hesiod
Virgil
Maha Bharata } Epitomized in Talboys Wheeler's
Ramayana } History of India, vols. i. and ii.
The Shahnameh
The Nibelungenlied
Malory's Morte d'Arthur

The Sheking
Kalidasa's Sakuntala or The Lost Ring
Æschylus' Prometheus
      Trilogy of Orestes
Sophocles' Œdipus
Euripides' Medea
Aristophanes' The Knights and Clouds
Horace

Chaucer's Canterbury Tales (perhaps in Morris' edition; or, if expurgated, in C. Clarke's, or Mrs. Haweis')
Shakespeare
Milton's Paradise Lost, Lycidas, Comus, and the shorter poems
Dante's Divina Commedia
Spenser's Fairie Queen

Dryden's Poems
Scott's Poems
Wordsworth (Mr. Arnold's selection)
Pope's Essay on Criticism
    Essay on Man
    Rape of the Lock
Burns
Byron's Childe Harold
Gray

Herodotus
Xenophon's Anabasis and Memorabilia
Thucydides
Tacitus' Germania
Livy
Gibbon's Decline and Fall
Hume's History of England
Grote's History of Greece
Carlyle's French Revolution
Green's Short History of England
Lewes' History of Philosophy

Arabian Nights
Swift's Gulliver's Travels
Defoe's Robinson Crusoe
Goldsmith's Vicar of Wakefield
Cervantes' Don Quixote
Boswell's Life of Johnson
Molière
Schiller's William Tell
Sheridan's The Critic, School for Scandal, and The Rivals
Carlyle's Past and Present

Bacon's Novum Organum
Smith's Wealth of Nations (part of)

Mill's Political Economy
Cook's Voyages
Humboldt's Travels
White's Natural History of Selborne
Darwin's Origin of Species
      Naturalist's Voyage
Mill's Logic

Bacon's Essays
Montaigne's Essays
Hume's Essays
Macaulay's Essays
Addison's Essays
Emerson's Essays
Burke's Select Works
Smiles' Self-Help

Voltaire's Zadig and Micromegas
Goethe's Faust, and Autobiography
Thackeray's Vanity Fair
      Pendennis
Dickens' Pickwick
      David Copperfield
Lytton's Last Days of Pompeii
George Eliot's Adam Bede
Kingsley's Westward Ho!
Scott's Novels

CHAPTER V.

THE BLESSING OF FRIENDS.

"They seem to take away the sun from the world who withdraw friendship from life; for we have received nothing better from the Immortal Gods, nothing more delightful."—CICERO.

MOST of those who have written in praise of books have thought they could say nothing more conclusive than to compare them to friends.

"All men," said Socrates, "have their different objects of ambition—horses, dogs, money, honor, as the case may be; but for his own part he would rather have a good friend than all these put together." And again, men know "the number of their other possessions, although they might be very numerous, but of their friends, though but few, they were not only ignorant of the number, but even when they attempted to reckon it to such as asked them, they set aside again some that they had previously counted among their friends; so little did they allow their friends to occupy their thoughts. Yet in comparison with what possession, of all others, would not a good friend appear far more valuable?"

"As to the value of other things," says Cicero, "most men differ; concerning friendship all have the same opinion. What can be more foolish than, when men are possessed of great influence by their wealth, power, and resources, to procure other things which are bought by money—horses, slaves, rich apparel, costly vases—and not to procure friends, the most valuable and fairest furniture of life?" And yet, he continues, "every man can tell how many goats or sheep he possesses, but not how many friends." In the choice, moreover, of a dog or of a horse, we exercise the greatest care: we inquire into its pedigree, its training and character, and yet we too often leave the selection of our friends, which is of infinitely greater importance—by whom our whole life will be more or less influenced either for good or evil—almost to chance.

It is no doubt true, as the *Autocrat of the Breakfast Table* says, that all men are bores except when we want them. And Sir Thomas Browne quaintly observes that "unthinking heads who have not learnt to be alone, are a prison to themselves if they be not with others; whereas, on the contrary, those whose thoughts are in a fair and hurry within, are sometimes fain to retire into company to be out of the crowd of themselves." Still I do not quite understand Emerson's idea that "men descend to meet." In another place, indeed, he qualifies the statement, and says, "Almost all people descend to meet." Even so I should venture to question it, especially considering the context. "All association," he adds, "must be a compromise, and, what is worse, the very flower and aroma of the flower of each of the beautiful natures disappears as they approach each other." What a sad thought! Is it really so; need it be so? And if it were, would friends be any real advantage? I should have thought that the influence of friends was exactly the reverse: that the flower of a beautiful nature would expand, and the colors grow brighter, when stimulated by the warmth and sunshine of friendship.

It has been said that it is wise always to treat a friend, remembering that he may become an enemy, and an enemy, remembering that he may become a friend; and whatever may be thought of the first part of the adage, there is certainly much wisdom in the latter. Many people seem to take more pains and more pleasure in making enemies, than in making friends. Plutarch, indeed, quotes with approbation the advice of Pythagoras "not to shake hands with too many," but as long as friends are well chosen, it is true rather that

> "He who has a thousand friends,
> Has never a one to spare,
> And he who has one enemy,
> Will meet him everywhere,"

and unfortunately, while there are few great friends there is no little enemy.

I guard myself, however, by saying again—As long as they are well chosen. One is thrown in life with a great many people who, though not actively bad, though they may not wilfully lead us astray, yet take no pains with themselves, neglect their own minds, and direct the conversation to petty puerilities or mere gossip; who do not seem to realize that conversation may by a little effort be made most instructive and delightful, without being in any way pedantic; or, on the other hand, may be allowed to drift into a mere morass of muddy thought and weedy words. There is hardly anyone from whom we may not learn much, if only they will trouble themselves to tell us. Nay, even if they teach us nothing, they may help us by the stimulus of intelligent questions, or the warmth of sympathy. But if they do neither, then indeed their companionship, if companionship it can be called, is mere waste of time, and of such we may well say, "I do desire that we be better strangers."

Much certainly of the happiness and purity of our lives depends on our making a wise choice of our companions and friends. If our friends are badly chosen they will inevitably drag us down; if well they will raise us up. Yet many people seem to trust in this matter to the chapter of accident. It is well and right, indeed, to be courteous and considerate to every one with whom we are brought into contact, but to choose them as real friends is another matter. Some seem to make a man a friend, or try to do so, because he lives near, because he is in the same business, travels on the same line of railway, or for some other trivial reason. There cannot be a greater mistake. These are only, in the words of Plutarch, "the idols and images of friendship."

To be friendly with every one is another matter; we must remember that there is no little enemy, and those who have ever really loved any one will have some tenderness for all. There is indeed some good in most men. "I have heard much," says Mr. Nasmyth in his charming autobiography, "about the ingratitude and selfishness of the world. It may have been my good fortune, but I have never experienced either of these unfeeling conditions." Such also has been my own experience.

> "Men talk of unkind hearts, kind deeds
> With coldness still returning.
> Alas! the gratitude of men
> Has oftener left me mourning."

I cannot, then, agree with Emerson that "we walk alone in the world. Friends such as we desire are dreams and fables. But a sublime hope cheers ever the faithful heart, that elsewhere in other regions of the universal power souls are now acting, enduring, and daring, which can love us, and which we can love."

No doubt, much as worthy friends add to the happiness and value of life, we must in the main depend on ourselves, and every one is his own best friend or worst enemy.

Sad, indeed, is Bacon's assertion that " there is little friendship in the world, and least of all between equals, which was wont to be magnified. That that is, is between superior and inferior, whose fortunes may comprehend the one to the other." But this can hardly be taken as his deliberate opinion, for he elsewhere says, " but we may go farther, and affirm most truly, that it is a mere and miserable solitude to want true friends, without which the world is but a wilderness." Not only, he adds, does friendship introduce "daylight in the understanding out of darkness and confusion of thoughts;" it "maketh a fair day in the affections from storm and tempests:" in consultation with a friend a man "tosseth his thoughts more easily; he marshalleth them more orderly; he seeth how they look when they are turned into words; finally, he waxeth wiser than himself, and that more by an hour's discourse than by a day's meditation."

. . . " But little do men perceive what solitude is, and how far it extendeth, for a crowd is not company, and faces are but a gallery of pictures, and talk but a tinkling cymbal where there is no love."

With this last assertion I cannot altogether concur. Surely even strangers may be most interesting! and many will agree with Dr. Johnson when, describing a pleasant evening, he summed it up— "Sir, we had a good talk."

Epictetus gives excellent advice when he dissuades from conversation on the very subjects most commonly chosen, and advises that it should be on " none of the common subjects—not about gladiators, nor horse-races, nor about athletes, nor about eating or drinking, which are the usual subjects; and especially not about men, as blaming them;" but when he adds, " or praising them," the injunction seems to me of doubtful value. Surely Marcus Aurelius more wisely advises that " when thou wishest to delight thyself, think of the virtues of those who live with thee; for instance, the activity of one, and the modesty of another, and the liberality of a third, and some other good quality of a fourth. For nothing delights so much as the examples of the virtues, when they are exhibited in the morals of those who live with us and present themselves in abundance, as far as is possible. Wherefore we must keep them before us." Yet how often we know merely the sight of those we call our friends, or the sound of their voices, but nothing whatever of their mind or soul.

We must, moreover, be as careful to keep friends as to make them. If every one knew what one said of the other, Pascal assures us that " there would not be four friends in the world." This I hope and think is too strong, but at any rate try to be one of the four. And when you have made a friend, keep him. Hast thou a friend, says an Eastern proverb, " visit him often, for thorns and brushwood obstruct the road which no one treads."

The affections should not be mere "tents of a night."

Still less does Friendship confer any privilege to make ourselves disagreeable. Some people never seem to appreciate their friends till they have lost them. Anaxagoras described the Mausoleum as the ghost of wealth turned into stone.

"But he who has once stood beside the grave to look back on the companionship which has been for ever closed, feeling how impotent *then* are the wild love and the keen sorrow, to give one instant's pleasure to the pulseless heart, or atone in the lowest measure to the departed spirit for the hour of unkindness, will scarcely for the future incur that debt to the heart which can only be discharged to the dust."[1]

Death, indeed, cannot sever friendship. "Friends," says Cicero, "though absent, are still present; though in poverty they are rich; though weak, yet in the enjoyment of health; and, what is still more difficult to assert, though dead they are alive." This seems a paradox, yet is there not much truth in his explanation? "To me, indeed, Scipio still lives, and will always live; for I love the virtue of that man, and that worth is not yet extinguished. . . . Assuredly of all things that either fortune or time has bestowed on me, I have none which I can compare with the friendship of Scipio."

[1] Ruskin.

If, then, we choose our friends for what they are, not for what they have, and if we deserve so great a blessing, then they will be always with us, preserved in absence, and even after death, in the "amber of memory."

CHAPTER VI.

THE VALUE OF TIME.

Each day is a little life.

ALL other good gifts depend on time for their value. What are friends, books, or health, the interest of travel or the delights of home, if we have not time for their enjoyment? Time is often said to be money, but it is more—it is life; and yet many who would cling desperately to life, think nothing of wasting time.

Ask of the wise, says Schiller in Lord Sherbrooke's translation,

> "The moments we forego
> Eternity itself cannot retrieve."

And, in the words of Dante,

> "For who knows most, him loss of time most grieves."

Not that a life of drudgery should be our ideal. Far from it. Time spent in innocent and rational enjoyments, in healthy games, in social and family intercourse, is well and wisely spent. Games not only keep the body in health, but give a command over the muscles and limbs which cannot be overvalued. Moreover, there are temptations which strong exercise best enables us to resist.

It is the idle who complain they cannot find time to do that which they fancy they wish. In truth, people can generally make time for what they choose to do; it is not really the time but the will that is wanting: and the advantage of leisure is mainly that we may have the power of choosing our own work, not certainly that it confers any privilege of idleness.

"Time travels in divers paces with divers persons. I'll tell you who time ambles withal, who time trots withal, who time gallops withal, and who he stands still withal." [1]

For it is not so much the hours that tell, as the way we use them.

> "Circles are praised, not that excel
> In largeness, but th' exactly framed;
> So life we praise, that doth excel
> Not in much time, but acting well." [2]

"Idleness," says Jeremy Taylor, "is the greatest prodigality in the world; it throws away that which is invaluable in respect of its present use, and irreparable when it is past, being to be recovered by no power of art or nature."

Life must be measured rather by depth than by

[1] Shakespeare.   [2] Waller.

length, by thought and action rather than by time. "A counted number of pulses only," says Pater, "is given to us of a variegated, aromatic, life. How may we see in them all that is to be seen by the finest senses? How can we pass most swiftly from point to point, and be present always at the focus where the greatest number of vital forces unite in their purest energy? To burn always with this hard gem-like flame, to maintain this ecstasy, is success in life. Failure is to form habits, for habit is relation to a stereotyped world: . . . while all melts under our feet, we may well catch at any exquisite passion, or any contribution to knowledge, that seems, by a lifted horizon, to set the spirit free for a moment."

I would not quote Lord Chesterfield as generally a safe guide, but there is certainly much shrewd wisdom in his advice to his son with reference to time. "Every moment you now lose, is so much character and advantage lost; as, on the other hand, every moment you now employ usefully, is so much time wisely laid out, at prodigious interest."

And again, "It is astonishing that any one can squander away in absolute idleness one single moment of that small portion of time which is allotted to us in the world . . . Know the true value of time; snatch, seize, and enjoy every moment of it."

"Are you in earnest? seize this very minute,
What you can do, or think you can, begin it."[1]

[1] *Faust.*

There is a Turkish proverb that the Devil tempts the Idle man, but the Idle man tempts the Devil. I remember, says Hilliard, "a satirical poem, in which the Devil is represented as fishing for men, and adapting his bait to the tastes and temperaments of his prey; but the idlers were the easiest victims, for they swallowed even the naked hook."

The mind of the idler indeed preys upon itself. "The human heart is like a millstone in a mill; when you put wheat under it, it turns and grinds and bruises the wheat to flour; if you put no wheat, it still grinds on—and grinds itself away." [1]

It is not work, but care, that kills, and it is in this sense, I suppose, that we are told to "take no thought for the morrow." To "consider the lilies of the field, how they grow; they toil not, neither do they spin: and yet even Solomon, in all his glory, was not arrayed like one of these. Wherefore, if God so clothe the grass of the field, which to-day is, and to-morrow is cast into the oven, shall he not much more clothe you, O ye of little faith?" It would indeed be a mistake to suppose that lilies are idle or imprudent. On the contrary, plants are most industrious, and lilies store up in their complex bulbs a great part of the nourishment of one year to quicken the growth of the next. Care, on the other hand, they certainly know not. [2]

[1] Luther.
[2] The word used μεριμνήσητε is translated in Liddell and Scott "to be anxious about, to be distressed in mind, to be cumbered with many cares."

"Hours have wings, fly up to the author of time, and carry news of our usage. All our prayers cannot entreat one of them either to return or slacken his pace. The misspents of every minute are a new record against us in heaven. Sure if we thought thus, we should dismiss them with better reports, and not suffer them to fly away empty, or laden with dangerous intelligence. How happy is it when they carry up not only the messages, but the fruits of good, and stay with the Ancient of Days to speak for us before His glorious throne!"[1]

Time is often said to fly; but it is not so much the time that flies; as we that waste it, and wasted time is worse than no time at all; "I wasted time," Shakespeare makes Richard II. say, "and now doth time waste me."

"He that is choice of his time," says Jeremy Taylor, "will also be choice of his company, and choice of his actions; lest the first engage him in vanity and loss, and the latter, by being criminal, be a throwing his time and himself away, and a going back in the accounts of eternity."

The life of man is seventy years, but how little of this is actually our own. We must deduct the time required for sleep, for meals, for dressing and undressing, for exercise, etc., and then how little remains really at our own disposal!

"I have lived," said Lamb, "nominally fifty years, but deduct from them the hours I have

[1] Milton.

lived for other people, and not for myself, and you will find me still a young fellow."

The hours we live for other people, however, are not those that should be deducted, but rather those which benefit neither oneself nor any one else; and these, alas! are often very numerous.

"There are some hours which are taken from us, some which are stolen from us, and some which slip from us."[1] But however we may lose them, we can never get them back. It is wonderful, indeed, how much innocent happiness we thoughtlessly throw away. An Eastern proverb says that calamities sent by heaven may be avoided, but from those we bring on ourselves there is no escape.

Some years ago I paid a visit to the principal lake villages of Switzerland in company with a distinguished archæologist, M. Morlot. To my surprise I found that his whole income was £100 a year, part of which, moreover, he spent in making a small museum. I asked him whether he contemplated accepting any post or office, but he said certainly not. He valued his leisure and opportunities as priceless possessions far more than silver or gold, and would not waste any of his time in making money.

Time indeed, is a sacred gift, and each day is a little life. Just think of our advantages here in London! We have access to the whole literature of the world; we may see in our National Gallery

[1] Seneca.

the most beautiful productions of former generations, and in the Royal Academy and other galleries the works of the greatest living artists. Perhaps there is no one who has ever found time to see the British Museum thoroughly. Yet consider what it contains; or rather, what does it not contain? The most gigantic of living and extinct animals; the marvellous monsters of geological ages; the most beautiful birds, shells, and minerals; precious stones and fragments from other worlds; the most interesting antiquities; curious and fantastic specimens illustrating different races of men; exquisite gems, coins, glass, and china; the Elgin marbles; the remains of the Mausoleum; of the temple of Diana of Ephesus; ancient monuments ot Egypt and Assyria; the rude implements of our predecessors in England, who were coeval with tne hippopotamus and rhinoceros, the musk-ox, and the mammoth; and beautiful specimens of Greek and Roman art.

Suffering may be unavoidable, but no one has any excuse for being dull. And yet some people *are* dull. They talk of a better world to come, while whatever dulness there may be here is all their own. Sir Arthur Helps has well said: "What! dull, when you do not know what gives its loveliness of form to the lily, its depth of color to the violet, its fragrance to the rose; when you do not know in what consists the venom of the adder, any more than you can imitate the glad movements of the dove. What! dull, when earth, air, and water are all alike mysteries to you, and when as you stretch out your hand you do not touch anything the properties of which you have mastered; while all the time Nature is inviting you to talk earnestly with her, to understand her, to subdue her, and to be blessed by her! Go away, man; learn something, do something, understand something, and let me hear no more of your dulness."

CHAPTER VII.

THE PLEASURES OF TRAVEL.

"I am a part of all that I have seen."—TENNYSON.

I AM sometimes disposed to think that there are few things in which we of this generation enjoy greater advantages over our ancestors than in the increased facilities of travel; but I hesitate to say this, not because our advantages are not great, but because I have already made the same remark with reference to several other aspects of life.

The very word "travel" is suggestive. It is a form of "travail"—excessive labor; and, as Skeat observes, it forcibly recalls the toil of travel in olden days. How different things are now!

It is sometimes said that every one should travel on foot "like Thales, Plato, and Pythagoras"; we are told that in these days of railroads people rush through countries and see nothing. It may be so, but that is not the fault of the railways. They confer upon us the inestimable advantage of being able, so rapidly and with so little fatigue, to visit countries which were much less accessible to our ancestors. What a blessing it is that not our own islands only—our smiling fields and rich woods, the mountains that are full of peace and the rivers of joy, the lakes and heaths and hills, castles and cathedrals, and many a spot immortalized in the history of our country:—not these only, but the sun and scenery of the South, the Alps the palaces of Nature, the blue Mediterranean, and the cities of Europe, with all their memories and treasures, are now brought within a few hours of us.

Surely no one who has the opportunity should omit to travel. The world belongs to him who has seen it. "But he that would make his travels delightful must first make himself delightful."[1]

According to the old proverb, "the fool wanders, the wise man travels." Bacon tells us that "the things to be seen and observed are the courts of princes, especially when they give audience to ambassadors; the courts of justice while they sit and hear causes; and so of consistories ecclesiastic; the churches and monasteries, with the monuments which are therein extant; the walls and fortifications of cities and towns; and so the havens and harbors, antiquities and ruins, libraries, colleges, disputations and lectures, when any are; shipping and navies; houses and gardens of state and pleasure near great cities; armories, arsenals, magazines, exchanges, burses, warehouses, exercises of horsemanship, fencing, training of soldiers,

[1] Seneca.

and the like ; comedies, such whereunto the better sort of persons do resort ; treasuries of jewels and robes ; cabinets and rarities ; and, to conclude, whatsoever is memorable in the places where they go."

But this depends on the time at our disposal, and the object with which we travel. If we can stay long in any one place Bacon's advice is no doubt excellent; but for the moment I am thinking rather of an annual holiday, taken for the sake of rest and health ; for fresh air and exercise rather than for study. Yet even so, if we have eyes to see we cannot fail to lay in a stock of new ideas as well as a store of health.

We may have read the most vivid and accurate description, we may have pored over maps and plans and pictures, and yet the reality will burst on us like a revelation. This is true not only of mountains and glaciers, of palaces and cathedrals, but even of the simplest examples.

For instance, like every one else, I had read descriptions and seen photographs and pictures of the Pyramids. Their form is simplicity itself. I do not know that I could put into words any characteristic of the original for which I was not prepared. It was not that they were larger; it was not that they differed in form, in color, or situation. And yet, the moment I saw them, I felt that my previous impression had been but a faint shadow of the reality. The actual sight seemed to give life to the idea.

Every one who has been in the East will agree that a week of oriental travel brings out, with more than stereoscopic effect, the pictures of patriarchal life as given us in the Old Testament. And what is true of the Old Testament is true of history generally. To those who have been in Athens or Rome, the history of Greece or Italy becomes far more interesting; while, on the other hand, some knowledge of the history and literature enormously enhances the interest of the scenes themselves.

Good descriptions and pictures, however, help us to see much more than we should perhaps perceive for ourselves. It may even be doubted whether some persons do not derive a more correct impression from a good drawing or description, which brings out the salient points, than they would from actual, but unaided, inspection. The idea may gain in accuracy, in character, and even in detail, more than it misses in vividness. But, however this may be, for those who cannot travel, descriptions and pictures have an immense interest; while to those who *have* traveled, they will afford an inexhaustible delight in reviving the memories of beautiful scenes and interesting expeditions.

It is really astonishing how little most of us see of the beautiful world in which we live. Mr. Norman Lockyer tells me that while traveling on a scientific mission in the Rocky Mountains, he was astonished to meet an aged French Abbé, and could not help showing his surprise. The Abbé observed this, and in the course of conversation explained his presence in that distant region.

"You were," he said, "I easily saw, surprised to find me here. The fact is, that some months ago I was very ill. My physicians gave me up: one morning I seemed to faint and thought that I was already in the arms of the Bon Dieu. I fancied one of the angels came and asked me, 'Well, M. l'Abbé, and how did you like the beautiful world you have just left?' And then it occurred to me that I who had been all my life preaching about heaven, had seen almost nothing of the world in which I was living. I determined therefore, if it pleased Providence to spare me, to see something of this world; and so here I am."

Few of us are free, however much we might wish it, to follow the example of the worthy Abbé. But although it may not be possible for us to reach the Rocky Mountains, there are other countries nearer home which most of us might find time to visit.

Though it is true that no descriptions can come near the reality, they may at least persuade us to give ourselves this great advantage. Let me then try to illustrate this by pictures in words, as realized by one of our most illustrious countrymen; I will select references to foreign countries only, not that we have not equal beauties here, but because everywhere in England one feels oneself at home.

The following passage from Tyndall's *Hours of*

Exercise in the Alps, is almost as good as an hour in the Alps themselves :

"I looked over this wondrous scene toward Mont Blanc, the Grand Combin, the Dent Blanche, the Weisshorn, the Dom, and the thousand lesser peaks which seem to join in the celebration of the risen day. I asked myself, as on previous occasions, How was this colossal work performed? Who chiselled these mighty and picturesque masses out of a mere protuberance of the earth? And the answer was at hand. Ever young, ever mighty—with the vigor of a thousand worlds still within him—the real sculptor was even then climbing up the eastern sky. It was he who raised aloft the waters which cut out these ravines; it was he who planted the glaciers on the mountain slopes, thus giving gravity a plough to open out the valleys; and it is he who, acting through the ages, will finally lay low these mighty monuments, rolling them gradually seaward, sowing the seeds of continents to be; so that the people of an older earth may see mould spread, and corn wave over the hidden rocks which at this moment bear the weight of the Jungfrau." And the Alps lie within twenty-four hours of London!

Tyndall's writings also contain many vivid descriptions of glaciers; those "silent and solemn causeways . . . broad enough for the march of an army in line of battle and quiet as a street of tombs in a buried city."[1] I do not, however,

[1] Ruskin.

borrow from him or from any one else any description of glaciers, for they are so unlike anything else, that no one who has not seen, can possibly visualize them.

The history of European rivers yet remains to be written, and is most interesting. They did not always run in their present courses. The Rhone, for instance, appears to have been itself a great traveler. At least there seems reasons to believe that the upper waters of the Valais fell at first into the Danube, and so into the Black Sea; subsequently joined the Rhine and the Thames, and so ran far north over the plains which once connected the mountains of Scotland and of Norway—to the Arctic Ocean; and to have only comparatively of late years adopted their present course into the Mediterranean.

But, however this may be, the Rhine of Germany and the Rhine of Switzerland are very unlike. The catastrophe of Schaffhausen seems to alter the whole character of the river, and no wonder. "Stand for half an hour," says Ruskin, "beside the Fall of Schaffhausen, on the north side where the rapids are long, and watch how the vault of water first bends, unbroken, in pure polished velocity, over the arching rocks at the brow of the cataract, covering them with a dome of crystal twenty feet thick, so swift that its motion is unseen except when a foam globe from above darts over it like a falling star; . . . and how ever and anon, startling you with its white flash, a jet of spray leaps hissing out of the fall, like a rocket, bursting in the wind and driven away in dust, filling the air with light; and how, through the curdling wreaths of the restless crushing abyss below, the blue of the water, paled by the foam in its body, shows purer than the sky through white raincloud; . . . their dripping masses lifted at intervals, like sheaves of loaded corn, by some stronger gush from the cataract, and bowed again upon the mossy rocks as its roar dies away."

But much as we may admire the majestic grandeur of a mighty river, either in its eager rush or its calmer moments, there is something which fascinates even more in the free life, the young energy, the sparkling transparence, and merry music of smaller streams.

"The upper Swiss valleys," as the same great Seer says, "are sweet with perpetual streamlets, that seem always to have chosen the steepest places to come down, for the sake of the leaps, scattering their handfuls of crystal this way and that, as the winds take them, with all the grace, but with none of the formalism, of fountains . . . until at last . . . they find their way down to the turf, and lose themselves in that, silently; with quiet depth of clear water furrowing among the grass blades, and looking only like their shadow, but presently emerging again in little startled gushes and laughing hurries, as if they had remembered suddenly that the day was too short for them to get down the hill."

How vividly does Symonds bring before us the sunny shores of the Mediterranean, which he loves so well, and the contrast between the scenery of the North and the South.

"In northern landscapes the eye travels through vistas of leafy boughs to still, secluded crofts and pastures, where slow-moving oxen graze. The mystery of dreams and the repose of meditation haunt our massive bowers. But in the South, the lattice-work of olive boughs and foliage scarcely veils the laughing sea and bright blue sky, while the hues of the landscape find their climax in the dazzling radiance of the sun upon the waves, and the pure light of the horizon. There is no concealment and no melancholy here. Nature seems to hold a never-ending festival and dance, in which the waves and sunbeams and shadows join. Again, in northern scenery, the rounded forms of full-foliaged trees suit the undulating country, with its gentle hills and brooding clouds; but in the South the spiky leaves and sharp branches of the olive carry out the defined outlines which are everywhere observable through the broader beauties of mountain and valley and sea-shore. Serenity and intelligence characterize this southern landscape, in which a race of splendid men and women lived beneath the pure light of Phœbus, their ancestral god. Pallas protected them, and golden Aphrodite favored them with beauty. Olives are not, however, by any means the only trees which play a part in idyllic scenery. The tall stone pine is even more important. . . . Near Massa, by Sorrento, there are two gigantic pines so placed that, lying on the grass beneath them, one looks on Capri rising from the sea, Baiae, and all the bay of Naples sweeping round to the base of Vesuvius. Tangled growths of olives, and rose-trees fill the garden-ground along the shore, while far away in the distance pale Inarime sleeps, with her exquisite Greek name, a virgin island on the deep.

"On the wilder hills you find patches of ilex and arbutus glowing with crimson berries and white waxen bells, sweet myrtle rods and shafts of bay, frail tamarisk and tall tree-heaths that wave their frosted boughs above your head. Nearer the shore the lentisk grows, a savory shrub, with cytisus and aromatic rosemary. Clematis and polished garlands of tough sarsaparilla wed the shrubs with clinging, climbing arms; and here and there in sheltered nooks the vine shoots forth luxuriant tendrils bowed with grapes, stretching from branch to branch of mulberry or elm, flinging festoons on which young loves might sit and swing, or weaving a lattice-work of leaves across the open shed. Nor must the sounds of this landscape be forgotten,— sounds of bleating flocks, and murmuring bees, and nightingales, and doves that moan, and running streams, and shrill cicadas, and hoarse frogs, and whispering pines. There is not a single detail which a patient student may not verify from Theocritus.

"Then too it is a landscape in which sea and

country are never sundered. The higher we climb upon the mountain-side the more marvellous is the beauty of the sea, which seems to rise as we ascend, and stretch into the sky. Sometimes a little flake of blue is framed by olive boughs, sometimes a turning in the road reveals the whole broad azure calm below. Or, after toiling up a steep ascent we fall upon the undergrowth of juniper, and lo! a double sea, this way and that, divided by the sharp spine of the jutting hill, jewelled with villages along its shore, and smiling with fair islands and silver sails."

To many of us the mere warmth of the South is a blessing and a delight. The very thought of it is delicious. I have read over again and again Wallace's graphic description of a tropical sunrise —of the "sun of the early morning that turneth all into gold."[1]

"Up to about a quarter past five o'clock," he says, "the darkness is complete; but about that time a few cries of birds begin to break the silence of night, perhaps indicating that signs of dawn are perceptible in the eastern horizon. A little later the melancholy voices of the goatsuckers are heard, varied croakings of frogs, the plaintive whistle of mountain thrushes, and strange cries of birds or mammals peculiar to each locality. About half-past five the first glimmer of light becomes perceptible; it slowly becomer lighter, and then increases so rapidly that at about a quarter to six it seems

[1] Morris.

full daylight. For the next quarter of an hour this changes very little in character; when, suddenly, the sun's rim appears above the horizon, decking the dew-laden foliage with glittering gems sending gleams of golden light far into the woods, and waking up all nature to life and activity. Birds chirp and flutter about, parrots scream, monkeys chatter, bees hum among the flowers, and gorgeous butterflies flutter lazily along or sit with full expanded wings exposed to the warm and invigorating rays. The first hour of morning in the equatorial regions possesses a charm and a beauty that can never be forgotten. All nature seems refreshed and strengthened by the coolness and moisture of the past night, new leaves and buds unfold almost before the eye, and fresh shoots may often be observed to have grown many inches since the preceding day. The temperature is the most delicious conceivable. The slight chill of early dawn, which was itself agreeable, is succeeded by an invigorating warmth; and the intense sunshine lights up the glorious vegetation of the tropics, and realizes all that the magic art of the painter or the glowing words of the poet have pictured as their ideals of terrestrial beauty."

Or take Dean Stanley's description of the colossal statues of Amenophis III., the Memnon of the Greeks, at Thebes—"The sun was setting, the African range glowed red behind them; the green plain was dyed with a deeper green beneath them, and the shades of evening veiled the vast rents and fissures in their aged frames. As I looked back at them in the sunset, and they rose up in front of the background of the mountain, they seemed, indeed, as if they were part of it,— as if they belonged to some natural creation."

But I must not indulge myself in more quotations, though it is difficult to stop. Such extracts recall the memory of many glorious days: for the advantages of travel last through life; and often, as we sit at home, "some bright and perfect view of Venice, of Genoa, or of Monte Rosa comes back on you, as full of repose as a day wisely spent in travel."[1]

So far is a thorough love and enjoyment of travel from interfering with the love of home, that perhaps no one can thoroughly enjoy his home who does not sometimes wander away. They are like exertion and rest, each the complement of the other; so that, though it may seem paradoxical, one of the greatest pleasures of travel is the return; and no one who has not roamed abroad, can realize the devotion which the wanderer feels for Domiduca—the sweet and gentle goddess who watches over our coming home.

[1] Helps.

CHAPTER VIII.

THE PLEASURES OF HOME.

"There's no place like Home."—*Old English Song.*

IT may well be doubted which is more delightful, —to start for a holiday which has been fully earned, or to return home from one which has been thoroughly enjoyed; to find oneself, with renewed vigor, with a fresh store of memories and ideas, back once more by one's own fireside, with one's family, friends, and books.

"To sit at home," says Leigh Hunt, "with an old folio (?) book of romantic yet credible voyages and travels to read, an old bearded traveller for its hero, a fireside in an old country house to read it by, curtains drawn, and just wind enough stirring out of doors to make an accompaniment to the billows or forests we are reading of—this surely is one of the perfect moments of existence."

It is no doubt a great privilege to visit foreign countries; to travel say in Mexico or Peru, or to cruise among the Pacific Islands; but in some respects the narratives of early travellers, the histories of Prescott or the voyages of Captain Cook, are even more interesting; describing to us, as they do, a state of society which was then so unlike ours, but which has now been much changed and Europeanized.

Thus we may make our daily travels interesting, even though, like those of the Vicar of Wakefield, all our adventures are by our own fireside, and all our migrations from one room to another.

Moreover, even if the beauties of home are humble, they are still infinite, and a man " may lie in his bed, like Pompey and his sons, in all quarters of the earth."[1]

It is, then, wise to " cultivate a talent very fortunate for a man of my disposition, that of travelling in my easy chair; of transporting myself, without stirring from my parlor, to distant places and to absent friends; of drawing scenes in my mind's eye; and of peopling them with the groups of fancy, or the society of remembrance."[2]

We may indeed secure for ourselves endless variety without leaving our own firesides.

In the first place, the succession of seasons multiplies every home. How different is the view from our windows as we look on the tender green of spring, the rich foliage of summer, the glorious tints of autumn, or the delicate tracery of winter.

Our climate is so happy, that even in the worst months of the year, " calm mornings of sunshine visit us at times, appearing like glimpses of departed spring amid the wilderness of wet and windy

[1] Sir T. Browne.   [2] Mackenzie, *The Lounger*.

days that lead to winter. It is pleasant, when these interludes of silver light occur, to ride into the woods and see how wonderful are all the colors of decay. Overhead, the elms and chestnuts hang their wealth of golden leaves, while the beeches darken into russet tones, and the wild cherry glows like blood-red wine. In the hedges crimson haws and scarlet hips are wreathed with hoary clematis or necklaces of coral briony-berries; the brambles burn with many-colored flames; the dog-wood is bronzed to purple; and here and there the spindle-wood puts forth its fruit, like knots of rosy buds, on delicate frail twigs. Underneath lie fallen leaves, and the brown brake rises to our knees as we thread the forest paths."[1]

Nay, every day gives us a succession of glorious pictures in never-ending variety. It is remarkable how few people seem to derive any pleasure from the beauty of the sky. Gray, after describing a sunrise—how it began with a slight whitening, just tinged with gold and blue, lit up all at once by a little line of insufferable brightness which rapidly grew to half an orb, and so to a whole one too glorious to be distinctly seen—adds, "I wonder whether any one ever saw it before. I hardly believe it." [2]

No doubt from the dawn of poetry, the splendors of the morning and evening skies have delighted all those who have eyes to see. But we are especially indebted to Ruskin for enabling us more

[1] J. A. Symonds.   [2] Gray's Letters.

vividly to realize these glorious sky pictures. As he says, in language almost as brilliant as the sky itself, the whole heaven, "from the zenith to the horizon, becomes one molten, mantling sea of color and fire; every block bar turns into massy gold, every ripple and wave into unsullied, shadowless crimson, and purple, and scarlet, and colors for which there are no words in language, and no ideas in the mind—things which can only be conceived while they are visible; the intense hollow blue of the upper sky melting through it all, showing here deep and pure, and lightness; there, modulated by the filmy, formless body of the transparent vapor, till it is lost imperceptibly in its crimson and gold."

It is in some cases indeed "not color but conflagration," and though the tints are richer and more varied toward morning and at sunset, the glorious kaleidoscope goes on all day long. Yet "it is a strange thing how little in general people know about the sky. It is the part of creation in which Nature has done more for the sake of pleasing man, more for the sole and evident purpose of talking to him, and teaching him, than in any other of her works, aud it is just the part in which we least attend to her. There are not many of her other works in which some more material or essential purpose than the mere pleasing of man is not answered by every part of their organization; but every essential purpose of the sky might, so far as we know, be answer, if once in three days, or thereabouts, a great, ugly, black rain-cloud were brought up over the blue, and everything well watered, and so all left blue again till next time, with perhaps a film of morning and evening mist for dew. And instead of this, there is not a moment of any day of our lives when Nature is not producing scene after scene, picture after picture, glory after glory, and working still upon such exquisite and constant principles of the most perfect beauty, that it is quite certain it is all done for us, and intended for our perpetual pleasure."[1]

Nor does the beauty end with the day. " It is nothing to sleep under the canopy of heaven, where we have the globe of the earth for our place of repose, and the glories of the heavens for our spectacle?"[2] For my part I always regret the custom of shutting up our rooms in the evening, as though there was nothing worth seeing outside. What, however, can be more beautiful than to " look how the floor of heaven is thick inlaid with patines of bright gold," or to watch the moon journeying in calm and silver glory through the night. And even if we do not feel that " the man who has seen the rising moon break out of the clouds at midnight, has been present like an Archangel at the creation of light and of the world,"[3] still " the stars say something significant to all of us: and each man has a whole hemisphere of them, if he will but look up, to counsel and befriend him";[4] for it is not so much, as Helps elsewhere observes,

[1] Ruskin. [2] Seneca. [3] Emerson. [4] Helps.

"in guiding us over the seas of our little planet, but out of the dark waters of our own perturbed minds, that we may make to ourselves the most of their significance." Indeed,

> "How beautiful is night!
> A dewy freshness fills the silent air;
> No mist obscures, nor cloud, nor speck, nor stain,
>   Breaks the serene of heaven:
> In full-orbed glory yonder moon divine
> Rolls through the dark blue depths;
>   Beneath her steady ray
>   The desert circle spreads,
> Like the round ocean, girdled with the sky;
>   How beautiful is night!" [1]

I have never wondered at those who worshipped the sun and moon.

On the other hand, when all outside is dark and cold; when perhaps

> "Outside fall the snowflakes lightly;
>   Through the night loud raves the storm;
> In my room the fire glows brightly,
>   And 'tis cosy, silent, warm.

> "Musing sit I on the settle
>   By the firelight's cheerful blaze,
> Listening to the busy kettle
>   Humming long forgotten lays." [2]

For after all the true pleasures of home are not without, but within; and "the domestic man who

[1] Southey.   [2] Heine, trans. by E. A. Bowring.

loves no music so well as his own kitchen clock and the airs which the logs sing to him as they burn on the hearth, has solaces which others never dream of."[1]

We love the ticking of the clock, and the flicker of the fire, like the sound of the cawing of rooks, not so much for any beauty of their own as for their associations.

It is a great truth that when we retire into ourselves we can call up what memories we please.

> "How dear to this heart are the scenes of my childhood,
> When fond recollection recalls them to view.—
> The orchard, the meadow, the deep-tangled wildwood
> And every lov'd spot which my infancy knew."[2]

It is not so much the

> "Fireside enjoyments,
> And *all the comforts* of the lowly roof,"[3]

but rather, according to the higher and better ideal of Keble,

> "Sweet is the smile of home; the mutual look,
> When hearts are of each other sure;
> Sweet all the joys that crowd the household nook,
> The haunt of all affections pure."

In ancient times, not only among savage races, but even among the Greeks themselves, there seems to have been but little family life.

[1] Emerson. [2] Woodworth. [3] Cowper.

What a contrast was the home life of the Greeks, as it seems to have been, to that, for instance, described by Cowley—a home happy " in books and gardens," and above all, in a

> " Virtuous wife, where thou dost meet
> Both pleasures more refined and sweet;
> The fairest garden in her looks
> And in her mind the wisest books."

No one who has ever loved mother or wife, sister or daughter, can read without astonishment and pity St. Chrysostom's description of woman as "a necessary evil, a natural temptation, a desirable calamity, a domestic peril, a deadly fascination, and a painted ill."

In few respects has mankind made a greater advance than in the relations of men and women. It is terrible to think how women suffer in savage life; and even among the intellectual Greeks, with rare exceptions, they seem to have been treated rather as housekeepers or playthings than as the Angels who make a Heaven of home.

The Hindoo proverb that you should "never strike a wife, even with a flower," though a considerable advance, tells a melancholy tale of what must previously have been.

In *The Origin of Civilization* I have given many cases showing how small a part family affection plays in savage life. Here I will only mention one case in illustration. The Algonquin (North America) language contained no word for " to love," so that when the missionaries translated the Bible into it they were obliged to invent one. What a life, and what a language, without love.

Yet in marriage even the rough passion of a savage may contrast favorably with any cold calculation, which, like the enchanted hoard of the Nibelungs, is almost sure to bring misfortune. In the Kalevala, the Finnish epic, the divine smith, Ilmarinnen, forges a bride of gold and silver for Wainamoinen, who was pleased at first to have so rich a wife, but soon found her intolerably cold, for, in spite of fires and furs, whenever he touched her she froze him.

Moreover, apart from mere coldness, how much we suffer from foolish quarrels about trifles; from mere misunderstandings; from hasty words thoughtlessly repeated, sometimes without the context or tone which would have deprived them of any sting. How much would that charity which "beareth all things, believeth all things, hopeth all things, endureth all things," effect to smooth away the sorrows of life and add to the happiness of home. Home indeed may be a sure haven of repose from the storms and perils of the world. But to secure this we must not be content to pave it with good intentions, but must make it bright and cheerful.

If our life be one of toil and of suffering, if the world outside be cold and dreary, what a pleasure to return to the sunshine of happy faces and the warmth of hearts we love.

CHAPTER IX.

SCIENCE.

> "Happy is he that findeth wisdom,
> And the man that getteth understanding:
> For the merchandise of it is better than silver,
> And the gain thereof than fine gold.
> She is more precious than rubies:
> And all the things thou canst desire are not to be
>   compared unto her.
> Length of days is in her right hand,
> And in her left hand riches and honor.
> Her ways are ways of pleasantness,
> And all her paths are peace."
> Proverbs of Solomon.

THOSE who have not tried for themselves can hardly imagine how much Science adds to the interest and variety of life. It is altogether a mistake to regard it as dry, difficult, or prosaic—much of it is as easy as it is interesting. A wise instinct of old united the prophet and the "seer." "The wise man's eyes are in his head, but the fool walketh in darkness." Technical works, descriptions of species, etc., bear the same relation to science as dictionaries do to literature.

Occasionally, indeed, Science may destroy some poetical myth of antiquity, such as the ancient Hindoo explanation of rivers, that "Indra dug out their beds with his thunderbolts, and sent them forth by long continuous paths;" but the real causes of natural phenomena are far more striking, and contain more true poetry, than those which have occurred to the untrained imagination of mankind.

In endless aspects science is as wonderful and interesting as a fairy tale.

> " There are things whose strong reality
> Outshines our fairyland; in shape and hues
> More beautiful than our fantastic sky,
> And the strange constellations which the Muse
> O'er her wild universe is skillful to diffuse."[1]

Mackay justly exclaims:

> " Blessings on Science! When the earth seemed old,
> When Faith grew doting, and our reason cold,
> 'Twas she discovered that the world was young,
> And taught a language to its lisping tongue."

Botany, for instance, is by many regarded as a dry science. Yet though without it we may admire flowers and trees, it is only as strangers, only as one may admire a great man or a beautiful woman in a crowd. The botanist, on the contrary

[1] Byron.

—nay, I will not say the botanist, but one with even a slight knowledge of that delightful science—when he goes out into the woods, or into one of those fairy forests which we call fields, finds himself welcomed by a glad company of friends, every one with something interesting to tell. Dr. Johnson said that, in his opinion, when you had seen one green field you had seen all; and a greater even than Johnson—Socrates—the very type of intellect without science, said he was always anxious to learn, and from fields and trees he could learn nothing.

It has, I know, been said that botanists

"Love not the flower they pluck and know it not.
And all their botany is but Latin names."

Contrast this, however, with the language of one who would hardly claim to be a master in botany, though he is certainly a loving student. "Consider," says Ruskin, "what we owe to the meadow grass, to the covering of the dark ground by that glorious enamel, by the companies of those soft, countless, and peaceful spears of the field! Follow but for a little time the thought of all that we ought to recognize in those words. All spring and summer is in them—the walks by silent scented paths, the rest in noonday heat, the joy of the herds and flocks, the power of all shepherd life and meditation; the life of the sunlight upon the world, falling in emerald streaks and soft blue shadows, when else it would have struck on the dark mould or scorching dust; pastures beside the pacing brooks, soft banks and knolls of lowly hills, thymy slopes of down overlooked by the blue line of lifted sea; crisp lawns all dim with early dew, or smooth in evening warmth of barred sunshine, dinted by happy feet, softening in their fall the sound of loving voices."

My own tastes and studies have led me mainly in the direction of Natural History and Archæology; but if you love one science, you cannot but feel intense interest in them all. How grand are the truths of Astronomy! Prudhomme, in a sonnet beautifully translated by Arthur O'Shaugnessy, has pictured an Observatory. He says—

> "'Tis late; the astronomer in his lonely height,
>   Exploring all the dark, descries afar
>   Orbs that like distant isles of splendor are."

He notices a comet, and calculating its orbit, finds that it will return in a thousand years—

> "The star will come. It dare not by one hour
>   Cheat Science, or falsify her calculation;
> Men will have passed, but, watchful in the tower,
>   Man shall remain in sleepless contemplation;
> And should all men have perished in their turn,
> Truth in their place would watch that star's return."

Ernest Rhys well says of a student's chamber—

> "Strange things pass nightly in this little room,
>   All dreary as it looks by light of day;
>   Enchantment reigns here when at evening play
>   Red fire-light glimpses through the pallid gloom."

And the true student, in Ruskin's words, stands on an eminence from which he looks back on the universe of God and forward over the generations of men.

Even if it be true that science was dry when it was buried in huge folios, that is certainly no longer the case now; and Lord Chesterfield's wise wish, that Minerva might have three graces as well as Venus, has been amply fulfilled.

The study of natural history indeed seems destined to replace the loss of what is, not very happily I think, termed "sport;" engraven in us as it is by the operation of thousands of years, during which man lived greatly on the produce of the chase. Game is gradually becoming "small by degrees and beautifully less." Our prehistoric ancestors hunted the mammoth, the woolly-haired rhinoceros, and Irish elk; the ancient Britons had the wild ox, the deer, and the wolf. We have still the pheasant, the partridge, the fox, and the hare; but even these are becoming scarcer, and must be preserved first, in order that they may be killed afterwards. Some of us even now—and more, no doubt, will hereafter—satisfy instincts, essentially of the same origin, by the study of birds, or insects, or even infusoria—of creatures which more than make up by their variety what they want in size.

Emerson avers that when a naturalist has "got all snakes and lizards in his phials, science has done for him also, and has put the man into a bottle." I do not deny that there are such cases, but they are quite exceptional. The true naturalist is no mere dry collector.

I cannot resist, although it is rather long, quoting the following description from Hudson and Gosse's beautiful work on the Rotifera:—

"On the Somersetshire side of the Avon, and not far from Clifton, is a little combe, at the bottom of which lies an old fish-pond. Its slopes are covered with plantations of beech and fir, so as to shelter the pond on three sides, and yet leave it open to the soft south-western breezes, and to the afternoon sun. At the head of the combe wells up a clear spring, which sends a thread of water, trickling through a bed of osiers, into the upper end of the pond. A stout stone wall has been drawn across the combe from side to side, so as to dam up the stream; and there is a gap in one corner through which the overflow finds its way in a miniature cascade, down into the lower plantation.

"If we approach the pond by the gamekeeper's path from the cottage above, we shall pass through the plantation, and come unseen right on the corner of the wall; so that one quiet step will enable us to see at a glance its whole surface, without disturbing any living thing that may be there.

"Far off at the upper end a water-hen is leading her little brood among the willows; on the fallen trunk of an old beech, lying half way across the pond, a vole is sitting erect, rubbing his right ear, and the splash of a beech husk just at our feet tells of a squirrel who is dining somewhere in the leafy crown above us.

"But see, the water-rat has spied us out, and is making straight for his hole in the bank, while the ripple above him is the only thing that tells of his silent flight. The water-hen has long ago got under cover, and the squirrel drops no more husks. It is a true Silent Pond, and without a sign of life.

"But if, retaining sense and sight, we could shrink into living atoms and plunge under the water, of what a world of wonders should we then form part! We should find this fairy kingdom peopled with the strangest creatures—creatures that swim with their hair, that have ruby eyes blazing deep in their necks, with telescopic limbs that now are withdrawn wholly within their bodies and now stretched out to many times their own length. Here are some riding at anchor, moored by delicate threads spun out from their toes; and there are others flashing by in glass armor, bristling with sharp spikes or ornamented with bosses and flowing curves; while fastened to a great stem is an animal convolvulus that, by some invisible power, draws a never-ceasing stream of victims into its gaping cup, and tears them to death with hooked jaws deep down within its body.

"Close by it, on the same stem, is something that looks like a filmy heart's-ease. A curious wheelwork runs round its four outspread petals; and a chain of minute things, living and dead, is winding in and out of their curves into a gulf at the back of the flower. What happens to them there we cannot see; for round the stem is raised a tube of golden-brown balls, all regularly piled on each other. Some creature dashes by, and like a flash the flower vanishes within its tube.

"We sink still lower, and now see on the bottom slow gliding lumps of jelly that thrust a shapeless arm out where they will, and grasping their prey with these chance limbs, wrap themselves round their food to get a meal; for they creep without feet, seize without hands, eat without mouths, and digest without stomachs."

Too many, however, still feel only in Nature that which we share "with the weed and the worm;" they love birds as boys do—that is, they love throwing stones at them; or wonder if they are good to eat, as the Esquimaux asked about the watch; or treat them as certain devout Afreedee villagers are said to have treated a descendant of the Prophet—killed him in order to worship at his tomb: but gradually we may hope that the love of Science—the notes "we sound upon the strings of nature" [1]—will become to more and more, as already it is to many, a "faithful and sacred element of human feeling."

Science summons us

"To that cathedral, boundless as our wonder,
Whose quenchless lamps the sun and moon supply;
Its choir the winds and waves, its organ thunder,
Its dome the sky." [2]

[1] Emerson.   [2] H. Smith.

Where the untrained eye will see nothing but mire and dirt, Science will often reveal exquisite possibilities. The mud we tread under our feet in the street is a grimy mixture of clay and sand, soot and water. Separate the sand, however, as Ruskin observes—let the atoms arrange themselves in peace according to their nature—and you have the opal. Separate the clay, and it becomes a white earth, fit for the finest porcelain; or if it still further purifies itself, you have a sapphire. Take the soot, and if properly treated it will give you a diamond. While, lastly, the water, purified and distilled, will become a dew-drop, or crystallize into a lovely star. Or, again, you may see as you will in any shallow pool either the mud lying at the bottom, or the image of the heavens above.

Nay, even if we imagine beauties and charms which do not really exist; still if we err at all it is better to do so on the side of charity; like Nasmyth, who tells us in his delightful autobiography, that he used to think one of his friends had a charming and kindly twinkle, and was one day surprised to discover that he had a glass eye.

But I should err indeed were I to dwell exclusively on science as lending interest and charm to our leisure hours. Far from this, it would be impossible to overrate the importance of scientific training on the wise conduct of life.

"Science," said the Royal Commission of 1861, "quickens and cultivates directly the faculty of observation, which in very many persons lies almost dormant through life, the power of accurate and rapid generalization, and the mental habit of method and arrangement; it accustoms young persons to trace the sequence of cause and effect; it familiarizes them with a kind of reasoning which interests them, and which they can promptly comprehend; and it is perhaps the best corrective for that indolence which is the vice of half-awakened minds, and which shrinks from any exertion that is not, like an effort of memory, merely mechanical."

Again, when we contemplate the grandeur of science, if we transport ourselves in imagination back into primeval times, or away into the immensity of space, our little troubles and sorrows seem to shrink into insignificance. "Ah, beautiful creations!" says Helps, speaking of the stars, "it is not in guiding us over the seas of our little planet, but out of the dark waters of our own perturbed minds, that we may make to ourselves the most of your significance." They teach, he tells us elsewhere, "something significant to all of us; and each man has a whole hemisphere of them, if he will but look up, to counsel and befriend him."

There is a passage in an address given many years ago by Professor Huxley to the South London Working Men's College which struck me very much at the time, and which puts this in language more forcible than any which I could use.

"Suppose," he said, "it were perfectly certain that the life and fortune of every one of us would, one day or other, depend upon his winning or losing a game of chess. Don't you think that we should all consider it to be a primary duty to learn at least the names and the moves of the pieces? Do you not think that we should look with a disapprobation amounting to scorn upon the father who allowed his son, or the State which allowed its members, to grow up without knowing a pawn from a knight? Yet it is a very plain and elementary truth that the life, the fortune, and the happiness of every one of us, and more or less of those who are connected with us, do depend upon our knowing something of the rules of a game infinitely more difficult and complicated than chess. It is a game which has been played for untold ages, every man and woman of us being one of the two players in a game of his or her own. The chessboard is the world, the pieces are the phenomena of the Universe, the rules of the game are what we call the laws of Nature. The player on the other side is hidden from us. We know that his play is always fair, just, and patient. But also we know to our cost that he never overlooks a mistake or makes the smallest allowance for ignorance. To the man who plays well the highest stakes are paid, with that sort of overflowing generosity which with the strong shows delight in strength. And one who plays ill is checkmated —without haste, but without remorse."

I have elsewhere endeavored to show the purifying and ennobling influence of science upon religion; how it has assisted, if indeed it may not claim the main share, in sweeping away the dark superstitions, the degrading belief in sorcery and witchcraft, and the cruel, however well-intentioned, intolerance which embittered the Christian world almost from the very days of the Apostles themselves. In this she has surely performed no mean service to religion itself. As Canon Fremantle has well and justly said, men of science, and not the clergy only, are ministers of religion.

Again, the national necessity for scientific education is imperative. We are apt to forget how much we owe to science, because so many of its wonderful gifts have become familiar parts of our everyday life, that their very value makes us forget their origin. At the recent celebration of the sexcentenary of Peterhouse College, near the close of a long dinner, Sir Frederick Bramwell was called on, some time after midnight, to return thanks for Applied Science. He excused himself from making a long speech on the ground that, though the subject was almost inexhaustible, the only illustration which struck him as appropriate under the circumstances was "the application of the domestic lucifer to the bedroom candle." One cannot but feel how unfortunate was the saying of the poet that

> "The light-outspeeding telegraph
> Bears nothing on its beam."

The report of the Royal Commission on Technical Instruction, which has recently been issued, teems with illustrations of the advantages afforded by technical instruction. At the same time, technical training ought not to begin too soon, for, as Bain truly observes, "in a right view of scientific education the first principles and leading examples, with select details, of all the great sciences, are the proper basis of the complete and exhaustive study of any single science." Indeed, in the words of Sir John Herschel, "it can hardly be pressed forcibly enough on the attention of the student of Nature, that there is scarcely any natural phenomenon which can be fully and completely explained in all its circumstances, without a union of several, perhaps of all, the sciences." The most important secrets of Nature are often hidden away in unexpected places. Many valuable substances have been discovered in the refuse of manufactories; and it was a happy thought of Glauber to examine what everybody else threw away. There is perhaps no nation the future happiness and prosperity of which depend more on science than our own. Our population is over 35,000,000, and is rapidly increasing. Even at present it is far larger than our acreage can support. Few people whose business does not lie in the study of statistics realize that we have to pay foreign countries no less than £140,000,000 a year for food. This, of course, we purchase mainly by manufactured articles. We hear now a great deal about depression of trade, and foreign, especially American, competition, which, let me observe, will be much keener a few years hence, when the United States have paid off their debt, and consequently reduced taxation.

But let us look forward a hundred years—no long time in the history of a nation. Our coal supplies will then be greatly diminished. The population of Great Britain doubles at the present rate of increase in about fifty years, so that we should, if the present rate continues, require to import over £400,000,000 a year in food. How, then, is this to be paid for? We have before us, as usual, three courses. The natural rate of increase may be stopped, which means suffering and outrage; or the population may increase, only to vegetate in misery and destitution; or, lastly, by the development of scientific training and appliances, they may probably be maintained in happiness and comfort. We have, in fact, to make our choice between science and suffering. It is only by wisely utilizing the gifts of science that we have any hope of maintaining our population in plenty and comfort. Science, however, will do this for us if we will only let her. She may be no Fairy Godmother indeed, but she will richly endow those who love her.

That discoveries, innumerable, marvellous, and fruitful, await the successful explorers of Nature no one can doubt. What would one not give for a Science primer of the next century? for, to paraphrase a well-known saying, even the boy at the plough will then know more of science than the wisest of our philosophers do now. Boyle entitled one of his essays "Of Man's great Ignorance of the Uses of Natural Things; or that there is no one thing in Nature whereof the uses to human life are yet thoroughly understood"—a saying which is still as true now as when it was written. And, lest I should be supposed to be taking too sanguine a view, let me give the authority of Sir John Herschel, who says: "Since it cannot but be that innumerable and most important uses remain to be discovered among the materials and objects already known to us, as well as among those which the progress of science must hereafter disclose, we may hence conceive a well-grounded expectation, not only of constant increase in the physical resources of mankind, and the consequent improvement of their condition, but of continual accession to our power of penetrating into the arcana of Nature and becoming acquainted with her highest laws."

Nor is it merely in a material point of view that science would thus benefit the nation. She will raise and strengthen the national, as surely as the individual, character. The great gift which Minerva offered to Paris is now freely tendered to all, for we may apply to the nation, as well as to the individual, Tennyson's noble lines:—

> "Self-reverence, self-knowledge, self-control:
> These three alone lead life to sovereign power,
> Yet not for power (power of herself
> Would come uncalled for), but to live by law;
> Acting the law we live by without fear."

"In the vain and foolish exultation of the heart," said John Quincy Adams, at the close of his final lecture on resigning his chair at Boston, "which the brighter prospects of life will sometimes excite, the pensive portress of Science shall call you to the sober pleasures of her holy cell. In the mortification of disappointment, her soothing voice shall whisper serenity and peace. In social converse with the mighty dead of ancient days, you will never smart under the galling sense of dependence upon the mighty living of the present age. And in your struggles with the world, should a crisis ever occur, when even friendship may deem it prudent to desert you, when priest and Levite shall come and look on you and pass by on the other side, seek refuge, my unfailing friends, and be assured you shall find it, in the friendship of Lælius and Scipio, in the patriotism of Cicero, Demosthenes, and Burke, as well as in the precepts and example of Him whose law is love, and who taught us to remember injuries only to forgive them."

Let me in conclusion quote the glowing description of our debt to science given by Archdeacon Farrar in his address at Liverpool College—testimony, moreover, all the more valuable, considering the source from which it comes.

"In this great commercial city," he said, "where you are surrounded by the triumphs of science and of mechanism—you, whose river is ploughed by the great steamships whose white wake has been called the fittest avenue to the palace front of a mercantile people—you know well that in the achievements of science there is not only beauty and wonder, but also beneficence and power. It is not only that she has revealed to us infinite space crowded with unnumbered worlds; infinite time peopled by unnumbered existences; infinite organisms hitherto invisible but full of delicate and iridescent loveliness; but also that she has been, as a great Archangel of Mercy, devoting herself to the service of man. She has labored, her votaries have labored, not to increase the power of despots or to add to the magnificence of courts, but to extend human happiness, to economize human effort, to extinguish human pain. Where of old, men toiled, half blinded and half naked, in the mouth of the glowing furnace to mix the white-hot iron, she now substitutes the mechanical action of the viewless air. She has enlisted the sunbeam in her service to limn for us, with absolute fidelity, the faces of the friends we love. She has shown the poor miner how he may work in safety, even amid the explosive fire-damp of the mine. She has, by her anæsthetics, enabled the sufferer to be hushed and unconscious while the delicate hand of some skilled operator cuts a fragment from the nervous circle of the unquivering eye. She points not to pyramids built during weary centuries by the sweat of miserable nations, but to the lighthouse and the steamship, to the railroad and the telegraph. She has restored eyes to the blind and hearing to the deaf. She has lengthened life, she has minimized danger, she has controlled madness, she has trampled on disease. And on all these grounds, I think that none of our sons should grow up wholly ignorant of studies which at once train the reason and fire the imagination, which fashion as well as forge, which can feed as well as fill the mind."

CHAPTER X.

EDUCATION.

"No pleasure is comparable to the standing upon the vantage ground of truth."—BACON.

"Divine Philosophy!
Not harsh and crabbed as dull fools suppose,
But musical as is Apollo's lute,
And a perpetual feast of nectar'd sweets
Where no crude surfeit reigns."—MILTON.

IT may seem rather surprising to include education among the pleasures of life; for in too many cases it is made odious to the young, and is supposed to cease with school; while, on the contrary, if it is to be really successful it must be suitable, and therefore interesting, to children, and must last through life. The very process of acquiring knowledge is a privilege and a blessing. It used to be said that there was no royal road to learning; it would be more true to say that the avenues leading to it are all royal.

"It is not," says Jeremy Taylor, "the eye that sees the beauties of heaven, nor the ear that hears the sweetness of music, or the glad tidings of a prosperous accident; but the soul that perceives all the relishes of sensual and intellectual perceptions: and the more noble and excellent the soul is, the greater and more savory are its perceptions. And if a child behold the rich ermine, or the diamonds of a starry night, or the order of the world, or hears the discourses of an apostle; because he makes no reflex act on himself and sees not what he sees, he can have but the pleasure of a fool or the deliciousness of a mule.

Herein lies the importance of education. I say education rather than instruction, because it is far more important to cultivate the mind than to store the memory. Studies are a means and not an end. "To spend too much time in studies is sloth; to use them too much for ornament is affectation; to make judgment wholly by their rules is the humor of a scholar: they perfect nature, and are perfected by experience. . . . Crafty men contemn studies, simple men admire them, and wise men use them."[1]

Moreover, though, as Mill says, "in the comparatively early state of human development in which we now live, a person cannot indeed feel that entireness of sympathy with all others which would make any real discordance in the general direction of their conduct in life impossible," yet education might surely do more to root in us the feeling of unity with our fellow-creatures. At any rate, if we do not study in this spirit, all our learning will but leave us as weak and sad as Faust.

[1] Bacon.

> "I've now, alas! Philosophy,
>   Medicine and Jurisprudence too,
> And to my cost Theology,
>   With ardent labor studied through,
> And here I stand, with all my lore
> Poor fool, no wiser than before."[1]

Our studies should be neither "a couch on which to rest; nor a cloister in which to promenade alone; nor a tower from which to look down on others; nor a fortress whence we may resist them; nor a workshop for gain and merchandise; but a rich armory and treasury for the glory of the creator and the ennoblement of life."[2]

For in the noble words of Epictetus, "you will do the greatest service to the state if you shall raise, not the roofs of the houses, but the souls of the citizens: for it is better that great souls should dwell in small houses rather than for mean slaves to lurk in great houses."

It is then of great importance to consider whether our present system of education is the one best calculated to fulfil these great objects. Does it really give that love of learning which is better than learning itself? Does all the study of the classics to which our sons devote so many years give any just appreciation of them; or do they not on leaving college too often feel with Byron—

> "Then farewell, Horace; whom I hated so!"

[1] Goethe.   [2] Bacon.

Too much concentration on any one subject is a great mistake, especially in early life. Nature herself indicates the true system, if we would but listen to her. Our instincts are good guides, though not infallible, and children will profit little by lessons which do not interest them. In cheerfulness, says Pliny, is the success of our studies—" studia hilaritate proveniunt"—and we may with advantage take a lesson from Theognis, who, in his Ode on the Marriage of Cadmus and Harmonia, makes the Muses sing:

> "What is good and fair,
>   Shall ever be our care;
>   Thus the burden of it rang,
>   That shall never be our care,
>   Which is neither good nor fair.
>   Such were the words your lips immortal sang."

There are some who seem to think that our educational system is as good as possible, and that the only remaining points of importance are the number of schools and scholars, the question of fees, the relation of voluntary and board schools, etc. "No doubt," says Mr. Symonds, in his *Sketches in Italy and Greece*, "there are many who think that when we not only advocate education but discuss the best sytem we are simply beating the air; that our population is as happy and cultivated as can be, and that no substantial advance is really possible. Mr. Galton, however, has expressed the opinion, and most of those who have written on the social condition of Athens seem to agree with him, that the population of Athens, taken as a whole, was as superior to us as we are to Australian savages."

That there is, indeed, some truth in this, probably no student of Greek history will deny. Why, then, should this be so? I cannot but think that our system of education is partly responsible.

Manual and science teaching need not in any way interfere with instruction in other subjects. Though so much has been said about the importance of science and the value of technical instruction, or of hand-training, as I should prefer to call it, it is unfortunately true that in our system of education, from the highest schools downward, both of them are sadly neglected, and the study of language reigns supreme.

This is no new complaint. Ascham, in *The Schoolmaster*, long ago lamented it; Milton, in his letter to Mr. Samuel Hartlib, complained "that our children are forced to stick unreasonably in these grammatick flats and shallows;" and observes that, "though a linguist should pride himself to have all the tongues Babel cleft the world into, yet, if he have not studied the solid things in them as well as the words and lexicons, he were nothing so much to be esteemed a learned man as any yeoman or tradesman competently wise in his mother dialect only;" and Locke said that "schools fit us for the university rather than for the world." Commission after commission, committee after committee, have reiterated the same complaint. How then do we stand now?

I see it indeed constantly stated that, even if the improvement is not so rapid as could be desired, still we are making considerable progress. But is this so? I fear not. I fear that our present system does not really train the mind, or cultivate the power of observation, or even give the amount of information which we may reasonably expect from the time devoted to it.

Sir M. E. Grant-Duff has expressed the opinion that a boy or girl of fourteen might reasonably be expected to "read aloud clearly and agreeably, to write a large distinct round hand, and to know the ordinary rules of arithmetic, especially compound addition—a by no means universal accomplishment; to speak and write French with ease and correctness, and have some slight acquaintance with French literature; to translate *ad aperturam libri* from an ordinary French or German book; to have a thoroughly good elementary knowledge of geography, under which are comprehended some notions of astronomy—enough to excite his curiosity; a knowledge of the very broadest facts of geology and history—enough to make him understand, in a clear but perfectly general way, how the larger features of the world he lives in, physical and political, came to be like what they are; to have been trained from earliest infancy to use his powers of observation on plants, or animals, or rocks, or other natural objects; and to have gathered a general acquaintance with what is most supremely good in that portion of the more important English classics which is suitable to his time of life; to have some rudimentary acquaintance with drawing and music."

To effect this, no doubt, "industry must be our oracle, and reason our Apollo," as Sir T. Browne says; but surely it is no unreasonable estimate; yet how far do we fall short of it? General culture is often deprecated because it is said that smatterings are useless. But there is all the difference in the world between having a smattering of, or being well grounded in, a subject. It is the latter which we advocate—to try to know, as Lord Brougham well said, "everything of something, and something of everything."

"It can hardly," says Sir John Herschel, "be pressed forcibly enough on the attention of the student of nature, that there is scarcely any natural phenomenon which can be fully and completely explained, in all its circumstances, without a union of several, perhaps of all, the sciences."

The present system in most of our public schools and colleges sacrifices everything else to classics and arithmetic. They are most important subjects, but ought not to exclude science and modern languages. Moreover, after all, our sons leave college unable to speak either Latin or Greek, and too often absolutely without any interest in classical history or literature. But the boy who has been educated without any training in science has grave reason to complain of "knowledge to one entrance quite shut out."

By concentrating the attention, indeed, so much on one or two subjects, we defeat our own object, and produce a feeling of distaste where we wish to create an interest.

Our great mistake in education is, as it seems to me, the worship of book-learning—the confusion of instruction and education. We strain the memory instead of cultivating the mind. The children in our elementary schools are wearied by the mechanical act of writing, and the interminable intricacies of spelling; they are oppressed by columns of dates, by lists of kings and places, which convey no definite idea to their minds, and have no near relation to their daily wants and occupations; while in our public schools the same unfortunate results are produced by the weary monotony of Latin and Greek grammar. We ought to follow exactly the opposite course with children—to give them a wholesome variety of mental food, and endeavor to cultivate their tastes, rather than to fill their minds with dry facts. The important thing is not so much that every child should be taught, as that every child should be given the wish to learn. What does it matter if the pupil know a little more or a little less? A boy who leaves school knowing much, but hating his lessons, will soon have forgotten almost all he ever learned; while another who had acquired a thirst for knowledge, even if he had learned little, would soon teach himself more than the first ever knew. Children are by nature eager for information. They are always putting questions. This ought to be encouraged. In fact, we may to a great extent trust to their instincts, and in that case they will do much to educate themselves. Too often, however, the acquirement of knowledge is placed before them in a form so irksome and fatiguing that all desire for information is choked, or even crushed out; so that our schools, in fact, become places for the discouragement of learning, and thus produce the very opposite effect from that at which we aim. In short, children should be trained to observe and to think, for in that way there would be opened out to them a source of the purest enjoyment for leisure hours, and the wisest judgment in the work of life.

Another point in which I venture to think that our system of education might be amended, is that it tends at present to give the impression that everything is known.

Dr. Busby is said to have kept his hat on in the presence of King Charles, that the boys might see what a great man he was. I doubt, however, whether the boys were deceived by the hat; and am very skeptical about Dr. Busby's theory of education.

Master John of Basingstoke, who was Archdeacon of Leicester in 1252, learned Greek during a visit to Athens, from Constantina, daughter of the Archbishop of Athens, and used to say afterwards that though he had studied well and diligently at the

University of Paris, yet he learned more from an Athenian maiden of twenty. We cannot all study so pleasantly as this, but the main fault I find with Dr. Busby's system is that it keeps out of sight the great fact of human ignorance.

Boys are given the impression that the masters know everything. If, on the contrary, the great lesson impressed on them was that what we know is as nothing to what we do not know, that the "great ocean of truth lies all undiscovered before us," surely this would prove a great stimulus, and many would be nobly anxious to enlarge the boundaries of human knowledge, and extend the intellectual kingdom of man. Philosophy, says Aristotle, begins in wonder, for Iris is the child of Thaumas.

Education ought not to cease when we leave school; but if well begun there, will continue through life.

Moreover, whatever our occupation or profession in life may be, it is most desirable to create for ourselves some other special interest. In the choice of a subject every one should consult his own instincts and interests. I will not attempt to suggest whether it is better to pursue art or science; whether we should study the motes in the sunbeam, or the heavenly bodies themselves. Whatever may be the subject of our choice, we shall find enough, and more than enough, to repay the devotion of a lifetime. Life no doubt is paved with enjoyments, but we must all expect times of anxiety, of suffering, and of sorrow; and when these come it is an inestimable comfort to have some deep interest which will, at any rate to some extent, enable us to escape from ourselves.

"A cultivated mind," says Mill—"I do not mean that of a philosopher, but any mind to which the fountains of knowledge have been opened, and which has been taught in any tolerable degree to exercise its faculties—will find sources of inexhaustible interest in all that surrounds it; in the objects of nature, the achievements of art, the imaginations of poetry, the incidents of history, the ways of mankind, past and present, and their prospects in the future. It is possible, indeed, to become indifferent to all this, and that too without having exhausted a thousandth part of it; but only when one has had from the beginning no moral or human interest in these things, and has sought in them only the gratification of curiosity."

I have been subjected to some good-natured banter for having said that I looked forward to a time when our artisans and mechanics would be great readers. But it is surely not unreasonable to regard our social condition as susceptible of great improvement. The spread of schools, the cheapness of books, the establishment of free libraries will, it may be hoped, exercise a civilizing and ennobling influence. They will even, I believe, do much to diminish poverty and suffering, so much of which is due to ignorance and to the want of interest and brightness in uneducated life. So far as our elementary schools are concerned, there is no doubt much difficulty in apportioning the National Grant without unduly stimulating mere mechanical instruction. But this is not the place to discuss the subject of religious or moral training, or the system of apportioning the grant.

If we succeed in giving the love of learning, the learning itself is sure to follow.

We should therefore endeavor to educate our children so that every country walk may be a pleasure; that the discoveries of science may be a living interest; that our national history and poetry may be sources of legitimate pride and rational enjoyment. In short, our schools, if they are to be worthy of the name—if they are to fulfil their high function—must be something more than mere places of dry study; they must train the children educated in them so that they may be able to appreciate and enjoy those intellectual gifts which might be, and ought to be, a source of interest and of happiness, alike to the high and to the low, to the rich and to the poor.

A wise system of education will at least teach us how little man yet knows, how much he has still to learn; it will enable us to realize that those who complain of the tiresome monotony of life have only themselves to blame; and that knowledge is pleasure as well as power. It will lead us all to try with Milton "to behold the bright countenance of truth in the quiet and still air of study," and to feel with Bacon that "no pleasure is comparable to the standing upon the vantage ground of truth."

We should then indeed realize in part, for as yet we cannot do so fully, the "sacred trusts of health, strength, and time," and how thankful we ought to be for the inestimable gift of life.

END OF PART I.

THE PLEASURES OF LIFE.

PART II.

PREFACE.

"And what is writ is writ—
Would it were worthier."

BYRON.

HEREWITH I launch the conclusion of my subject. Perhaps I am unwise in publishing a second part. The first was so kindly received that I am running a risk in attempting to add to it.

In the preface, however, to the first part I have expressed the hope that the thoughts and quotations in which I have found most comfort and delight, might be of use to others also.

In this my most sanguine hopes have been more than realized. Not only has the book passed through thirteen editions in less than two years, but the many letters which I have received have been most gratifying.

Two criticisms have been repeated by several of those who have done me the honor of noticing my previous volume. It has been said in the first place that my life has been exceptionally bright and full, and that I cannot therefore judge for others. Nor do I attempt to do so. I do not forget, I hope I am not ungrateful for, all that has been bestowed on me. But if I have been greatly favored, ought I not to be on that very account especially qualified to write on such a theme? Moreover, I have had,—who has not,—my own sorrows.

Again, some have complained that there is too much quotation—too little of my own. This I take to be in reality a great compliment. I have not striven to be original.

If, as I have been assured by many, my book have proved a comfort, and have been able to cheer in the hour of darkness, that is indeed an ample reward, and is the utmost I have ever hoped.

HIGH ELMS, DOWN,
  KENT, *April* 1889.

CHAPTER I.

AMBITION.

Fame is the spur that the clear spirit doth raise
(That last infirmity of noble minds)
To scorn delights and live laborious days."
>	MILTON.

CHAPTER I.

AMBITION.

IF fame be the last infirmity of noble minds, ambition is often the first; though, when properly directed, it may be no feeble aid to virtue.

Had not my youthful mind, says Cicero, "from many precepts, from many writings, drunk in this truth, that glory and virtue ought to be the darling, nay, the only wish in life; that, to attain these, the torments of the flesh, with the perils of death and exile, are to be despised; never had I exposed my person in so many encounters, and to these daily conflicts with the worst of men, for your deliverance. But, on this head, books are full; the voice of the wise is full; the examples of antiquity are full: and all these the night of barbarism had still enveloped, had it not been enlightened by the sun of science."

The poet tells us that

"The many fail: the one succeeds."[1]

But this is scarcely true. All succeed who deserve, though not perhaps as they hoped. An

[1] Tennyson.

honorable defeat is better than a mean victory, and no one is really the worse for being beaten, unless he loses heart. Though we may not be able to attain, that is no reason why we should not aspire.

I know, says Morris,

> "How far high failure overleaps the bound
> Of low successes."

And Bacon assures us that "if a man look sharp and attentively he shall see fortune; for though she is blind, she is not invisible."

To give ourselves a reasonable prospect of success we must realize what we hope to achieve; and then make the most of our opportunities. Of these the use of time is one of the most important. What have we to do with time, asks Oliver Wendell Holmes, but to fill it up with labor.

"At the battle of Montebello," said Napoleon, "I ordered Kellermann to attack with 800 horse, and with these he separated the 6000 Hungarian grenadiers before the very eyes of the Austrian cavalry. This cavalry was half a league off, and required a quarter of an hour to arrive on the field of action; and I have observed that it is always these quarters of an hour that decide the fate of a battle," including, we may add, the battle of life.

Nor must we spare ourselves in other ways, for

> "He who thinks in strife
> To earn a deathless fame, must do, nor ever care for
> life."[1]

[1] Beowulf.

In the excitement of the struggle, moreover, he will suffer comparatively little from wounds and blows which would otherwise cause intense suffering.

It is well to weigh scrupulously the object in view, to run as little risk as may be, to count the cost with care.

But when the mind is once made up, there must be no looking back, you must spare yourself no labor, nor shrink from danger.

> "He either fears his fate too much
> Or his deserts are small,
> That dares not put it to the touch
> To gain or lose it all." [1]

Glory, says Renan, "is after all the thing which has the best chance of not being altogether vanity." But what is glory?

Marcus Aurelius observes that "a spider is proud when it has caught a fly, a man when he has caught a hare, another when he has taken a little fish in a net, another when he has taken wild boars, another when he has taken bears, and another when he has taken Sarmatians;" [2] but this, if from one point of view it shows the vanity of fame, also encourages us with the evidence that every one may succeed if his objects are but reasonable.

[1] Montrose.
[2] He is referring here to one of his expeditions.

Alexander may be taken as almost a type of Ambition in its usual form, though carried to an extreme.

His desire was to conquer, not to inherit or to rule. When news was brought that his father Philip had taken some town, or won some battle, instead of appearing delighted with it, he used to say to his companions, "My father will go on conquering, till there be nothing extraordinary left for you and me to do."[1] He is said even to have been mortified at the number of the stars, considering that he had not been able to conquer one world. Such ambition is justly foredoomed to disappointment.

The remarks of Philosophers on the vanity of ambition refer generally to that unworthy form of which Alexander may be taken as the type—the idea of self-exaltation, not only without any reference to the happiness, but even regardless of the sufferings, of others.

"A continual and restless search after fortune," says Bacon, "takes up too much of their time who have nobler things to observe." Indeed he elsewhere extends this, and adds, "No man's private fortune can be an end any way worthy of his existence."

Goethe well observes that man "exists for culture; not for what he can accomplish, but for what can be accomplished in him."[2]

As regards fame we must not confuse name and

[1] Plutarch. [2] Emerson.

essence. To be remembered is not necessarily to be famous. There is infamy as well as fame; and unhappily almost as many are remembered for the one as for the other, and not a few for the mixture of both.

Who would not rather be forgotten, than recollected as Ahab or Jezebel, Nero or Commodus, Messalina or Heliogabalus, King John or Richard III.?

"To be nameless in worthy deeds exceeds an infamous history. The Canaanitish woman lives more happily without a name than Herodias with one; and who would not rather have been the good thief than Pilate?"[1]

Kings and Generals are often remembered as much for their deaths as for their lives, for their misfortunes as for their successes. The Hero of Thermopylæ was Leonidas, not Xerxes. Alexander's Empire fell to pieces at his death. Napoleon was a great genius, though no Hero. But what came of all his victories? They passed away like the smoke of his guns, and he left France weaker, poorer, and smaller than he found her. The most lasting result of his genius is no military glory, but the Code Napoléon.

A surer and more glorious title to fame is that of those who are remembered for some act of justice or self-devotion: the self-sacrifice of Leonidas, the good faith of Regulus, are the glories of history.

[1] Sir J. Browne.

In some cases where men have been called after places, the men are remembered, while the places are forgotten. When we speak of Palestrina or Perugino, of Nelson or Wellington, of Newton or Darwin, who remembers the towns? We think only of the men.

Goethe has been called the soul of his century.

It is true that we have but meagre biographies of Shakespeare or of Plato; yet how much we know about them.

Statesmen and Generals enjoy great celebrity during their lives. The newspapers chronicle every word and movement. But the fame of the Philosopher and Poet is more enduring.

Wordsworth deprecates monuments to Poets, with some exceptions, on this very account. The case of Statesmen, he says, is different. It is right to commemorate them because they might otherwise be forgotten; but Poets live in their books forever.

The real conquerors of the world indeed are not the generals but the thinkers; not Genghis Khan and Akbar, Rameses, or Alexander, but Confucius and Buddha, Aristotle, Plato, and Christ. The rulers and kings who reigned over our ancestors have for the most part long since sunk into oblivion —they are forgotten for want of some sacred bard to give them life—or are remembered, like Suddhodana and Pilate, from their association with higher spirits.

Such men's lives cannot be compressed into any biography. They lived not merely in their own generation, but for all time. When we speak of the Elizabethan period we think of Shakespeare and Bacon, Raleigh and Spenser. The ministers and secretaries of state, with one or two exceptions, we scarcely remember, and Bacon himself is recollected less as the Judge than as the Philosopher.

Morever, to what do Generals and Statesmen owe their fame? They were celebrated for their deeds, but to the Poet and the Historian they owe their fame, and to the Poet and Historian we owe their glorious memories and the example of their virtues.

> "Vixere fortes ante Agamemnona
> Multi; sed omnes illacrimabiles
> Urgentur ignotique longâ
> Nocte, carent quia vate sacro."

There were many brave men before Agamemnon, but their memory has perished because they were celebrated by no divine Bard. Montrose happily combined the two, when in "My dear and only love" he promises,

> "I'll make thee glorious by my pen,
> And famous by my sword."

It is remarkable, and encouraging, how many of the greatest men have risen from the lowest rank, and triumphed over obstacles which might well have seemed insurmountable; nay, even obscurity itself may be a source of honor. The very doubts as to Homer's birthplace have contributed to this glory, seven cities as we all know laying claim to the great poet—

"Smyrna, Chios, Colophon, Salamis, Rhodos, Argos, Athenæ."

To take men of Science only. Ray was the son of a blacksmith, Watt of a shipwright, Franklin of a tallow-chandler, Dalton of a handloom weaver, Fraünhofer of a glazier, Laplace of a farmer, Linnæus of a poor curate, Faraday of a blacksmith, Lamarck of a banker's clerk; Davy was an apothecary's assistant, Galileo, Kepler, Sprengel, Cuvier, and Sir W. Herschel were all children of very poor parents.

It is, on the other hand, sad to think how many of our greatest benefactors are unknown even by name. Who discovered the art of procuring fire? Prometheus is merely the personification of forethought. Who invented letters? Cadmus is a mere name.

These inventions, indeed, are lost in the mists of antiquity, but even as regards recent progress the steps are often so gradual, and so numerous, that few inventions can be attributed entirely, or even mainly, to any one person.

Columbus is said, and truly said, to have discovered America, though the Northmen were there before him.

We Englishmen have every reason to be proud of our fellow-countrymen. To take Philosophers and men of Science only, Bacon and Hobbes' Locke and Berkeley, Hume and Hamilton, will always be associated with the progress of human thought; Newton with gravitation, Adam Smith with Political Economy, Young with the undulatory theory of light, Herschel with the discovery of Uranus and the study of the star depths, Lord Worcester, Trevethick, and Watt with the steam-engine, Wheatstone with the electric telegraph, Jenner with the banishment of smallpox, Simpson with the practical application of anæsthetics, and Darwin with the creation of modern Natural History.

These men, and such as these, have made our history and moulded our opinions; and though during life they may have occupied, comparatively, an insignificant space in the eyes of their countrymen, they became at length an irresistible power, and have now justly grown to a glorious memory.

CHAPTER II.

WEALTH.

"The rich and poor meet together; the Lord is the maker of them all."—Proverbs of Solomon.

CHAPTER II.

WEALTH.

AMBITION often takes the form of a love of money. There are many who have never attempted Art or Music, Poetry or Science; but most people do something for a livelihood, and consequently an increase of income is not only acceptable in itself, but gives a pleasant feeling of success.

Doubt is often expressed whether wealth is any advantage. I do not myself believe that those who are born, as the saying is, with a silver spoon in their mouth, are necessarily any the happier for it. No doubt wealth entails almost more labor than poverty, and certainly more anxiety. Still it must, I think, be confessed that the possession of an income, whatever it may be, which increases somewhat as the years roll on, does add to the comfort of life.

Unquestionably the possession of wealth is by no means unattended by drawbacks. Money and the love of money often go together. The poor man, as Emerson says, is the man who wishes to be rich; and the more a man has, the more he often longs to be richer. Just as drinking often does but increase thirst; so in many cases the craving for riches does grow with wealth.

This is, of course, especially the case when money is sought for its own sake. Moreover, it is often easier to make money than to keep or to enjoy it. Keeping it is dull and anxious drudgery. The dread of loss may hang like a dark cloud over life. Apicius, when he squandered most of his patrimony, but had still 250,000 crowns left, committed suicide, as Seneca tells us, for fear he should die of hunger.

Wealth is certainly no sinecure. Moreover, the value of money depends partly on knowing what to do with it, partly on the manner in which it is acquired.

"Acquire money, thy friends say, that we also may have some. If I can acquire money and also keep myself modest, and faithful, and magnanimous, point out the way, and I will acquire it. But if you ask me to love the things which are good and my own, in order that you may gain things that are not good, see how unfair and unwise you are. For which would you rather have? Money, or a faithful and modest friend. . . .

"What hinders a man, who has clearly comprehended these things, from living with a light heart, and bearing easily the reins, quietly expecting everything which can happen, and enduring that which has already happened? Would you have me to bear poverty? Come, and you will know what poverty is when it has found one who can act well the part of a poor man."[1]

We must bear in mind Solon's answer to Crœsus, "Sir, if any other come that hath better iron than you, he will be master of all this gold."

Midas is another case in point. He prayed that everything he touched might be turned into gold, and this prayer was granted. His wine turned to gold, his bread turned to gold, his clothes, his very bed.

> "Attonitus novitate mali, divesque miserque,
>   Effugere optat opes, et quæ modo voverat, odit."

He is by no means the only man who has suffered from too much gold.

The real truth I take to be that wealth is not necessarily an advantage, but that whether it is so or not depends on the use we make of it. The same, however, might be said of most other opportunities and privileges; Knowledge and Strength, Beauty and Skill, may all be abused; if we neglect or misuse them we are worse off than if we had never had them. Wealth is only a disadvantage in the hands of those who do not know how to use it. It gives the command of so many other things—leisure, the power of helping friends, books, works of art, opportunities and means of travel.

It would, however, be easy to exaggerate the ad-

[1] Epictetus.

vantages of money. It is well worth having, and worth working for, but it does not requite too great a sacrifice; not indeed so great as is often offered up to it. A wise proverb tells us that gold may be bought too dear. If wealth is to be valued because it gives leisure, clearly it would be a mistake to sacrifice leisure in the struggle for wealth. Money has no doubt also a tendency to make men poor in spirit. But, on the other hand, what gift is there which is without danger?

Euripides said that money finds friends for men, and has great (he said the greatest) power among Mankind, cynically adding, "A mighty person indeed is a rich man, especially if his heir be unknown."

Bossuet tells us that " he had no attachment to riches, still if he had only what was barely necessary, he felt himself narrowed, and would lose more than half his talents."

Shelley was certainly not an avaricious man, and yet "I desire money," he said, "because I think I know the use of it. It commands labor, it gives leisure; and to give leisure to those who will employ it in the forwarding of truth is the noblest present an individual can make to the whole."

Many will have felt with Pepys when he quaintly and piously says, "Abroad with my wife, the first time that ever I rode in my own coach; which do make my heart rejoice and praise God, and pray him to bless it to me, and continue it."

This, indeed, was a somewhat selfish satisfaction. Yet the merchant need not quit nor be ashamed of his profession, bearing in mind only the inscription on the Church of St. Giacomo de Rialto at Venice: " Around this temple let the merchant's law be Just, his weight true, and his covenants faithful. "[1]

If life has been sacrificed to the rolling up of money for its own sake, the very means by which it was acquired will prevent its being enjoyed ; the chill of poverty will have entered into the very bones. The term Miser was happily chosen for such persons ; they are essentially miserable.

" A collector peeps into all the picture shops of Europe for a landscape of Poussin, a crayon sketch of Salvator ; but the Transfiguration, the Last Judgment, the Communion of St. Jerome, and what are as transcendent as these, are on the walls of the Vatican, the Uffizi, or the Louvre, where every footman may see them ; to say nothing of Nature's pictures in every street, of sunsets and sunrises every day, and the sculpture of the human body never absent. A collector recently bought at public auction in London, for one hundred and fifty-seven guineas, an autograph of Shakespeare : but for nothing a schoolboy can read Hamlet, and can detect secrets of highest concernment yet unpublished therein."[2] And yet " What hath the owner but the sight of it with his eyes."[3]

We are really richer than we think. We often hear of Earth hunger. People envy a great Land-

[1] Ruskin.   [2] Emerson.   [3] Solomon.

lord, and fancy how delightful it must be to possess a large estate. But, as Emerson says, " if you own land, the land owns you." Moreover, have we not all, in a better sense—have we not all thousands of acres of our own? The commons, and roads, and footpaths, and the seashore, our grand and varied coast—these are all ours. The seacoast has, moreover, two great advantages. In the first place, it is for the most part but little interfered with by man, and in the second it exhibits most instructively the forces of Nature. We are all great landed proprietors, if we only knew it. What we lack is not land, but the power to enjoy it. Moreover, this great inheritance has the additional advantage that it entails no labor, requires no management. The landlord has the trouble, but the landscape belongs to every one who has eyes to see it. Thus Kingsley called the heaths round Eversley his " winter garden ;" not because they were his in the eye of the law, but in that higher sense in which ten thousand persons may own the same thing.

CHAPTER III.

HEALTH.

"Health is best for mortal man; next beauty; thirdly, well gotten wealth; fourthly, the pleasures of youth among friends."

SIMONIDES.

CHAPTER III.

HEALTH.

BUT if there has been some difference of opinion as to the advantage of wealth, with reference to health all are agreed.

"Health," said Simonides long ago, "is best for mortal man; next beauty; thirdly, well gotten wealth; fourthly, the pleasure of youth among friends." "Life," says Longfellow, "without health is a burden, with health is a joy and gladness." Empedocles delivered the people of Selinus from a pestilence by draining a marsh, and was hailed as a Demigod. We are told that a coin was struck in his honor, representing the Philosopher in the act of staying the hand of Phœbus.

We scarcely realize, I think, how much we owe to Doctors. Our system of Medicine seems so natural and obvious that it hardly occurs to us as somewhat new and exceptional. When we are ill we send for a Physician; he prescribes some medicine; we take it, and pay his fee. But among the lower races of men pain and illness are often attributed to the presence of evil spirits. The Medicine Man is a Priest, or rather a Sorcerer, more than a true Doctor, and his effort is to exorcise the evil spirit.

In other countries where some advance has been made, a charm is written on a board, washed off, and drunk. In some cases the medicine is taken, not by the patient, but by the Doctor. Such a system, however, is generally transient; it is naturally discouraged by the Profession, and is indeed incompatible with a large practice. Even as regards the payment we find very different systems. The Chinese pay their medical man as long as they are well, and stop his salary as soon as they are ill. In ancient Egypt we are told that the patient feed the Doctor for the first few days, after which the Doctor paid the patient until he made him well. This is a fascinating system, but might afford too much temptation to heroic remedies.

On the whole our plan seems the best, though it does not offer adequate encouragement to discovery and research. We do not appreciate how much we owe to the discoveries of such men as Hunter and Jenner, Simpson and Lister. And yet in the matter of health we can generally do more for ourselves than the greatest Doctors can for us.

But if all are agreed as to the blessing of health, there are many who will not take the little trouble, or submit to the slight sacrifices, necessary to maintain it. Many, indeed, deliberately ruin their own health, and incur the certainty of an early grave, or an old age of suffering.

No doubt some inherit a constitution which renders health almost unattainable. Pope spoke of that long disease, his life. Many indeed may say, "I suffer, therefore I am." But happily these cases are exceptional. Most of us might be well, if we would. It is very much our own fault that we are ill. We do those things which we ought not to do, and we leave undone those things which we ought to have done, and then we wonder there is no health in us.

We all know that we can make ourselves ill, but few perhaps realize how much we can do to keep ourselves well. Much of our suffering is self-inflicted. It has been observed that among the ancient Egyptians the chief aim of life seemed to be to be well buried. Many, however, live even now as if this were the principal object of their existence.

Like Naaman, we expect our health to be the subject of some miraculous interference, and neglect the homely precautions by which it might be secured.

I am inclined to doubt whether the study of health is sufficiently impressed on the minds of those entering life. Not that it is desirable to potter over minor ailments, to con over books on illnesses, or experiment on ourselves with medicine. Far from it. The less we fancy ourselves ill, or bother about little bodily discomforts, the more likely perhaps we are to preserve our health.

It is, however, a different matter to study the general conditions of health. A well-known proverb tells us that every one is a fool or a physician at forty. Unfortunately, however, many persons are invalids at forty as well as physicians.

Ill-health, however, is no excuse for moroseness. If we have one disease we may at least congratulate ourselves that we are escaping all the rest. Sydney Smith, ever ready to look on the bright side of things, once, when borne down by suffering, wrote to a friend that he had gout, asthma, and seven other maladies, but was "otherwise very well;" and many of the greatest invalids have borne their sufferings with cheerfulness and good spirits.

It is said that the celebrated physiognomist, Campanella, could so abstract his attention from any sufferings of his body, that he was even able to endure the rack without much pain; and whoever has the power of concentrating his attention and controlling his will, can emancipate himself from most of the minor miseries of life. He may have much cause for anxiety, his body may be the seat of severe suffering, and yet his mind will remain serene and unaffected; he may triumph over care and pain.

But many have undergone much unnecessary suffering, and valuable lives have often been lost, through ignorance or carelessness. We cannot but fancy that the lives of many great men might have been much prolonged by the exercise of a little ordinary care.

If we take musicians only, what a grievous loss

to the world it is that Pergolesi should have died at twenty-six, Schubert at thirty-one, Mozart at thirty-five, Purcell at thirty-seven, and Mendelssohn at thirty-eight.

In the old Greek myth the life of Meleager was indissolubly connected by fate with the existence of a particular log of wood. As long as this was kept safe by Althæa, his mother, Meleager bore a charmed life. It seems wonderful that we do not watch with equal care over our body, on the state of which happiness so much depends.

The requisites of health are plain enough; regular habits, daily exercise, cleanliness, and moderation in all things—in eating as well as in drinking—would keep most people well.

I need not here dwell on the evils of drinking, but we perhaps scarcely realize how much of the suffering and ill-humor of life is due to over-eating. Dyspepsia, for instance, from which so many suffer, is in nine cases out of ten their own fault, and arises from the combination of too much food with too little exercise. To lengthen your life, says an old proverb, shorten your meals. Plain living and high thinking will secure health for most of us, though it matters, perhaps, comparatively little what a healthy man eats, so long as he does not eat too much.

Mr. Gladstone has told us that the splendid health he enjoys is greatly due to his having early learnt one simple physiological maxim, and laid it down as a rule for himself always to make twenty-five bites at every bit of meat.

> "Go to your banquet then, but use delight,
> So as to rise still with an appetite." [1]

No doubt, however, though the rule not to eat or drink too much is simple enough in theory, it is not quite so easy in application. There have been many Esaus who sold their birthright of health for a mess of pottage.

Moreover, it may seem paradoxical, but it is certainly true, that in the long run the moderate man will derive more enjoyment even from eating and drinking, than the glutton or the drunkard will ever obtain. They know not what it is to enjoy "the exquisite taste of common dry bread." [2]

And yet even if we were to consider merely the pleasure to be derived from eating and drinking, the same rule would hold good. A lunch of bread and cheese after a good walk is more enjoyable than a Lord Mayor's feast. Without wishing, like Apicius, for the neck of a stork, so that he might enjoy his dinner longer, we must not be ungrateful for the enjoyment we derive from eating and drinking, even though they be amongst the least æsthetic of our pleasures. They are homely, no doubt, but they come morning, noon, and night, and are not the less real because they have reference to the body rather than the soul.

[1] Herrick.   [2] Hamerton.

We speak truly of a healthy appetite, for it is a good test of our bodily condition; and indeed in some cases of our mental state also. That

> "There cometh no good thing
> Apart from toil to mortals,"

is especially true with reference to appetite; to sit down to a dinner, however simple, after a walk with a friend among the mountains or along the shore, is no insignificant pleasure.

Cheerfulness and good humor, moreover, during meals are not only pleasant in themselves, but conduce greatly to health.

It has been said that hunger is the best sauce, but most would prefer some good stories at a feast even to a good appetite; and who would not like to have it said of him, as of Biron by Rosaline—

> " A merrier man
> Within the limit of becoming mirth
> I never spent an hour's talk withal."

In the three great "Banquets" of Plato, Xenophon, and Plutarch, the food is not even mentioned.

In the words of the old Lambeth adage—

> "What is a merry man?
> Let him do what he can
> To entertain his guests
> With wine and pleasant jests,
> Yet if his wife do frown
> All merryment goes down."

What salt is to food, wit and humor are to comversation and literature. "You do not," an amusing writer in the *Cornhill* has said, "expect humor in Thomas à Kempis or Hebrew Prophets;" but we have Solomon's authority that there is a time to laugh, as well as to weep.

"To read a good comedy is to keep the best company in the world, when the best things are said, and the most amusing things happen." [1]

It is not without reason that every one resents the imputation of being unable to see a joke.

Laughter appears to be the special prerogative of man. The higher animals present us with proof of evident, if not highly developed reasoning power, but it is more than doubtful whether they are capable of appreciating a joke.

Wit, moreover, has solved many difficulties and decided many controversies.

"Ridicule shall frequently prevail,
And cut the knot when graver reasons fail." [2]

A careless song, says Walpole, with a little nonsense in it now and then, does not misbecome a monarch, but it is difficult now to realize that James I. should have regarded skill in punning in his selections of bishops and privy councillors.

The most wasted of all days, says Chamfort, is that on which one has not laughed.

It is, moreover, no small merit of laughter that

[1] Hazlitt. [2] Francis.

it is quite spontaneous. "You cannot force people to laugh; you cannot give a reason why they should laugh; they must laugh of themselves or not at all. . . . If we think we must not laugh, this makes our temptation to laugh the greater."[1] Humor is, moreover, contagious. A witty man may say, as Falstaff does of himself, "I am not only witty in myself, but the cause that wit is in other men."

But one may pharaphrase the well-known remark about port wine and say that some jokes may be better than others, but anything which makes one laugh is good. "After all," says Dryden, "it is a good thing to laugh at any rate; and if a straw can tickle a man, it is an instrument of happiness," and I may add, of health.

I have been told that in omitting any mention of smoking I was overlooking one of the real pleasures of life. Not being a smoker myself I cannot perhaps judge; much must depend on the individual temperament; to some nervous natures it certainly appears to be a great comfort; but I have my doubts whether smoking, as a general rule, does add to the pleasures of life. It must, moreover, detract somewhat from the sensitiveness of taste and of smell.

Those who live in cities may almost lay it down as a rule that no time spent out of doors is ever wasted. Fresh air is a cordial of incredible virtue; old families are in all senses county families, not town families; and those who prefer Homer

[1] Hazlitt.

and Plato and Shakespeare to hares and partridges and foxes must beware that they are not tempted to neglect this great requisite of our nature.

Most Englishmen, however, love open air, and it is probably true that most of us enjoy a game at cricket or golf more than looking at any of the old masters. The love of sport is engraven in the English character. As was said of William Rufus, "he loves the tall deer as he had been their father."

An Oriental traveler is said to have watched a game of cricket and been much astonished at hearing that many of those playing were rich men. He asked why they did not pay some poor people to do it for them.

Wordsworth made it a rule to go out every day, and he used to say that as he never consulted the weather, he never had to consult the physicians.

It always seems to be raining harder than it really is when you look at the weather through the window. Even in winter, though the landscape often seems cheerless and bare enough when you look at it from the fireside, still it is far better to go out, even if you have to brave the storm: when you are once out of doors the touch of earth and the breath of the fresh air gives you fresh life and energy. Men, like trees, live in great part on air.

After a gallop over the downs, a row on the river, a sea voyage, a walk by the seashore or in the woods

"The blue above, the music in the air,
The flowers upon the ground,"[1]

one feels as if one could say with Henry IV., "Je me porte comme le Ponte Neuf."

The Roman proverb that a child should be taught nothing which he cannot learn standing up, went no doubt into an extreme, but surely we fall into another when we act as if games were the only thing which boys could learn upon their feet.

The love of games among boys is certainly a healthy instinct, and though carried too far in some of our great schools, there can be no question that cricket and football, boating and hockey, bathing and birdnesting, are not only the greatest pleasures, but the best medicines for boys.

We cannot always secure sleep. When important decisions have to be taken, the natural anxiety to come to a right decision will often keep us awake. Nothing, however, is more conducive to healthy sleep than plenty of open air. Then indeed we can enjoy the fresh life of the early morning: " the breezy call of incense-bearing morn."[2]

"At morn the Blackcock trims his jetty wing,
'Tis morning tempts the linnet's blithest lay,
All nature's children feel the matin spring
Of life reviving with reviving day."

Epictetus described himself as "a spirit bearing about a corpse." That seems to me an ungrateful

[1] Trench.   [2] Gray.

description. Surely we ought to cherish the body, even if it be but a frail and humble companion. Do we not own to the eye our enjoyment of the beauties of this world and the glories of the Heavens; to the ear the voices of friends and all the delights of music; are not the hands most faithful and invaluable instruments, ever ready in case of need, ever willing to do our bidding; and even the feet bear us without a murmur along the roughest and stoniest paths of life.

With reasonable care, then, most of us may hope to enjoy good health. And yet what a marvellous and complex organization we have!

We are indeed fearfully and wonderfully made. It is

> "Strange that a harp of a thousand strings,
> Should keep in tune so long."

When we consider the marvellous complexity of our bodily organization, it seems a miracle that we should live at all; much more that the innumerable organs and processes should continue day after day and year after year with so much regularity and so little friction that we are sometimes scarcely conscious of having a body at all.

And yet in that body we have more than 200 bones, of complex and varied forms, any irregularity in, or injury to, which would of course grievously interfere with our movements.

We have over 500 muscles; each nourished by almost innumerable blood vessels, and regulated by nerves. One of our muscles, the heart, beats over 30,000,000 times in a year, and if it once stops, all is over.

In the skin are wonderfully varied and complex organs—for instance, over 2,000,000 perspiration glands, which regulate the temperature and communicate with the surface by ducts, which have a total length of some ten miles.

Think of the miles of arteries and veins, of capillaries and nerves; of the blood, with the millions of millions of blood corpuscles, each a microcosm in itself.

Think of the organs of sense,—the eye with its cornea and lens, vitreous humor, aqueous humor, and choroid, culminating in the retina, no thicker than a sheet of paper, and yet consisting of nine distinct layers, the innermost composed of rods and cones, supposed to be the immediate recipients of the undulations of light, and so numerous that in each eye the cones are estimated at over 3,000,000, the rods at over 30,000,000.

Above all, and most wonderful of all, the brain itself. Meinert has calculated that the gray matter of the convolutions alone contains no less than 600,000,000 cells; each cell consists of several thousand visible atoms, and each atom again of many millions of molecules.

And yet with reasonable care we can most of us keep this wonderful organization in health; so that it will work without causing us pain, or even discomfort, for many years; and we may hope that oven when old age comes

> "Time may lay his hand
> Upon your heart gently, not smiting it
> But as a harper lays his open palm
> Upon his harp, to deaden its vibrations."

CHAPTER IV.
LOVE.

"Love rules the court, the camp, the grove,
And men below and saints above;
For love is heaven and heaven is love."
                                          SCOTT.

CHAPTER IV.

LOVE.

LOVE is the light and sunshine of life. We are so constituted that we cannot fully enjoy ourselves, or anything else, unless some one we love enjoys it with us. Even if we are alone, we store up our enjoyment in hope of sharing it hereafter with those we love.

Love lasts through life, and adapts itself to every age and circumstance; in childhood for father and mother, in manhood for wife, in age for children, and throughout for brothers and sisters, relations and friends. The strength of friendship is indeed proverbial, and in some cases, as in that of David and Jonathan, is described as surpassing the love of women. But I need not now refer to it, having spoken already of what we owe to friends.

The goodness of Providence to man has been often compared to that of fathers and mothers for their children.

"Just as a mother, with sweet, pious face,
   Yearns toward her little children from her seat,
Gives one a kiss, another an embrace,
   Takes this upon her knees, that on her feet;

And while from actions, looks, complaints, pretences,
  She learns their feelings and their various will,
To this a look, to that a word, dispenses,
  And, whether stern or smiling, loves them still;—
So Providence for us, high, infinite,
  Makes our necessities its watchful task,
  Hearkens to all our prayers, helps all our wants,
And e'en if it denies what seems our right,
  Either denies because 'twould have us ask,
  Or seems but to deny, or in denying grants." [1]

Sir Walter Scott well says—

"And if there be on Earth a tear
From passion's dross [2] refined and clear,
'Tis that which pious fathers shed
Upon a duteous daughter's head."

Epaminondas is said to have given as his main reason for rejoicing at the victory of Leuctra, that it would give so much pleasure to his father and mother.

Nor must the love of animals be altogether omitted. It is impossible not to sympathize with the Savage when he believes in their immortality, and thinks that after death

"Admitted to that equal sky
His faithful dog shall bear him company." [3]

In the *Mahabharata*, the great Indian Epic, when the family of Pandavas, the heroes, at length

---

[1] *Filicaja.* Translated by Leigh Hunt.
[2] Not from passion itself.   [3] Pope.

reach the gates of heaven, they are welcomed themselves, but are told that their dog cannot come in. Having pleaded in vain, they turn to depart, as they say they can never leave their faithful companion. Then at the last moment the Angel at the door relents, and their Dog is allowed to enter with them.

We may hope the time will come when we shall learn

> "Never to blend our pleasures or our pride,
> With sorrow of the meanest thing that feels." [1]

But at the present moment I am speaking rather of the love which leads to marriage. Such love is the music of life, nay, "there is music in the beauty, and the silver note of love, far sweeter than the sound of any instrument." [2]

The Symposium of Plato contains an interesting and amusing disquisition on Love.

"Love," Phædrus is made to say, "will make men dare to die for their beloved—love alone: and women as well as men. Of this, Alcestis, the daughter of Pelias, is a monument to all Hellas; for she was willing to lay down her life on behalf of her husband, when no one else would, although he had a father and mother; but the tenderness of her love so far exceeded theirs, that she made them seem to be strangers in blood to their own son, and in name only related to him; and so

[1] Wordsworth. [2] Browne.

noble did this action of hers appear to the gods, as well as to men, that among the many who have done virtuously she is one of the very few to whom they have granted the privilege of returning to earth, in admiration of her virtue; such exceeding honor is paid by them to the devotion and virtue of love."

Agathon is even more eloquent—

Love " fills men with affection, and takes away their disaffection, making them meet together at such banquets as these. In sacrifices, feasts, dances, he is our lord—supplying kindness and banishing unkindness, giving friendship and forgiving anmity, the joy of the good, the wonder of the wise, the amazement of the gods, desired by those who have no part in him, and precious to those who have the better part in him; parent of delicacy, luxury, desire, fondness, softness, grace, regardful of the good, regardless of the evil. In every word, work, wish, fear—pilot, comrade, helper, savior; glory of gods and men, leader best and brightest: in whose footsteps let every man follow, sweetly singing in his honor that sweet strain with which love charms the souls of gods and men."

No doubt, even so there are two Loves, " one, the daughter of Uranus, who has no mother, and is the elder and wiser goddess; and the other, the daughter of Zeus and Dione, who is popular and common,"—but let us not examine too closely. Charity tells us even of Guinevere, "that while she lived, she was a good lover and therefore she had a good end." [1]

The origin of love has exercised philosophers almost as much as the origin of evil. The Symposium continues with a speech which Plato attributes in joke to Aristophanes, and of which Jowett observes that nothing in Aristophanes is more truly Aristophanic.

The original human nature, he says, was not like the present. The Primeval Man was round, [2] his back and sides forming a circle ; and he had four hands and four feet, one head with two faces, looking opposite ways, set on a round neck and precisely alike. He could walk upright as men now do, backward or forward as he pleased, and he could also roll over and over at a great rate, whirling round on his four hands and four feet, eight in all, like tumblers going over and over with their legs in the air; this was when he wanted to run fast. Terrible was their might and strength, and the thoughts of their hearts great, and they made an attack upon the gods; of them is told the tale of Otys and Ephialtes, who, as Homer says, dared to scale heaven, and would have laid hands upon the gods. Doubt reigned in the celestial councils. Should they kill them and annihilate the race with thunderbolts, as they had done the giants, then there would be an end of the sacrifices and worship which men offered to

[1] Malory, *Morte d' Arthur*.
[2] I avail myself of Dr. Jowett's translation.

them; but, on the other hand, the gods could not suffer their insolence to be unrestrained. At last, after a good deal of reflection, Zeus discovered a way. He said; "Methinks I have a plan which will humble their pride and mend their manners; they shall continue to exist, but I will cut them in two, which will have a double advantage, for it will halve their strength and we shall have twice as many sacrifices. They shall walk upright on two legs, and if they continue insolent and will not be quiet, I will split them again and they shall hop on a single leg." He spoke and cut men in two, "as you might split an egg with a hair." . . . After the division the two parts of man, each desiring his other half, came together. . . . So ancient is the desire of one another which is implanted in us, reuniting our original nature, making one of two, and healing the state of man. Each of us when separated is but the indenture of a man, having one side only, like a flat-fish and he is always looking for his other half.

And when one of them finds his other half, the pair are lost in amazement of love and friendship and intimacy, and one will not be out of the other's sight, as I may say, even for a minute: they will pass their whole lives together; yet they could not explain what they desire of one another. For the intense yearning which each of them has toward the other does not appear to be the desire of lover's intercourse, but of something else, which the soul of either evidently desires and cannot tell, and of which she has only a dark and doubtful presentiment.

However this may be, there is such instinctive insight in the human heart that we often form our opinion almost instantaneously, and such impressions seldom change, I might even say, they are seldom wrong. Love at first sight sounds like an imprudence, and yet is almost a revelation. It seems as if we were but renewing the relations of a previous existence.

> "But to see her were to love her,
> Love but her, and love for ever." [1]

Yet though experience seldom falsifies such a feeling, happily the reverse does not hold good. The deepest affection is often of slow growth. Many a warm love has been won by faithful devotion.

Montaigne indeed declares that "Few have married for love without repenting it." Dr. Johnson also maintained that marriages would generally be happier if they were arranged by the Lord Chancellor; but I do not think either Montaigne or Johnson were good judges. As Lancelot said to the unfortunate Maid of Astolat, "I love not to be constrained to love, for love must arise of the heart and not by constraint." [2]

Love defies distance and the elements; Sestos

---

[1] Burns.   [2] Malory, *Morte d' Arthur*.

and Abydos are divided by the sea, "but Love joined them by an arrow from his bow." [1]

Love can be happy anywhere. Byron wished

> "O that the desert were my dwelling-place,
> With one fair Spirit for my minister,
> That I might all forget the human race,
> And, hating no one, love but only her."

And many will doubtless have felt

> "O Love! what hours were thine and mine
> In lands of Palm and Southern Pine,
> In lands of Palm, of Orange blossom,
> Of Olive, Aloe, and Maize and Vine."

What is true of space holds good equally of time.

> "In peace, Love tunes the shepherd's reed·
> In war, he mounts the warrior's steed;
> In halls, in gay attire is seen;
> In hamlets, dances on the green.
> Love rules the court, the camp, the grove,
> And men below, and saints above;
> For love is heaven, and heaven is love." [2]

Even when, as among some Eastern races, Religion and Philosophy have combined to depress Love, truth reasserts itself in popular sayings, as for instance in the Turkish proverb, "All women are perfection, especially she who loves you."

[1] Symonds.   [2] Scott.

LOVE. 185

A French lady having once quoted to Abd-el-Kader the Polish proverb, "A woman draws more with a hair of her head than a pair of oxen well harnessed;" he answered with a smile, "The hair is unnecessary, woman is powerful as fate."

But we like to think of Love rather as the Angel of Happiness than as a ruling force: of the joy of home when "hearts are of each other sure."

> "It is the secret sympathy,
>   The silver link, the silken tie,
>   Which heart to heart, and mind to mind
>   In body and in soul can bind." [1]

What Bacon says of a friend is even truer of a wife; there is "no man that imparteth his joys to his friend, but he joyeth the more; and no man that imparteth his griefs to his friend, but he grieveth the less."

Let some one we love come near us and

> "At once it seems that something new or strange
>   Has passed upon the flowers, the trees, the ground;
>   Some slight but unintelligible change
>   On everything around." [2]

We might, I think, apply to love what Homer says of Fate:

> "Her feet are tender, for she sets her steps
>   Not on the ground, but on the heads of men."

[1] Scott. [2] Trench.

Love and Reason divide the life of man. We must give to each its due. If it is impossible to attain to virtue by the aid of Reason without Love, neither can we do so by means of Love alone without Reason.

Love, said Melanippides, "sowing in the heart of man the sweet harvest of desire, mixes the sweetest and most beautiful things together."

No one indeed could complain now, with Phædrus in Plato's Symposium, that Love has had no worshippers among the Poets. On the contrary, Love has brought them many of their sweetest inspirations; none perhaps nobler or more beautiful than Milton's description of Paradise:

> " With thee conversing, I forget all time,
> All seasons, and their change, all please alike.
> Sweet is the breath of morn, her rising sweet
> With charm of earliest birds; pleasant the sun
> When first on this delightful land he spreads
> His orient beams on herb, tree, fruit, and flower
> Glistering with dew, fragrant the fertile earth
> After soft showers; and sweet the coming on
> Of grateful evening mild; then silent night
> With this her solemn bird and this fair moon,
> And these the gems of heaven, her starry train:
> But neither breath of morn when she ascends
> With charm of earliest birds, nor rising sun
> On this delightful land, nor herb, fruit, flower
> Glistering with dew, nor fragrance after showers,
> Nor grateful evening mild, nor silent night
> With this her solemn bird, nor walk by moon
> Or glittering starlight, without thee is sweet."

Moreover, no one need despair of an ideal marriage. We unfortunately differ so much in our tastes; love does so much to create love, that even the humblest may hope for the happiest marriage if only he deserves it; and Shakespeare speaks, as he does so often, for thousands when he says

> "She is mine own,
> And I as rich in having such a jewel
> As twenty seas, if all their sands were pearls,
> The water nectar, and the rocks pure gold."

True love indeed will not be unreasonable or exacting.

> "Tell me not, sweet, I am unkind
>   That from the nursery
> Of thy chaste breast and quiet mind
>   To war and arms I fly.
> True! a new mistress now I chase,
>   The first foe in the field,
> And with a stronger faith embrace
>   A sword, a horse, a shield.
> Yet this inconstancy is such
>   As you too shall adore,
> I could not love thee, dear, so much,
>   Loved I not honor more." [1]

And yet

> "Alas! how light a cause may move
> Dissension between hearts that love!
> Hearts that the world in vain had tried,
> And sorrow but more closely tied,

[1] Lovelace.

>That stood the storm, when waves were rough,
>　Yet in a sunny hour fall off,
>Like ships that have gone down at sea,
>　When heaven was all tranquillity." [1]

For love is brittle. Do not risk even any little jar; it may be

>"The little rift within the lute,
>That by and by will make the music mute,
>And ever widening slowly silence all." [2]

Love is delicate; "Love is hurt with jar and fret," and you might as well expect a violin to remain in tune if roughly used, as Love to survive if chilled or driven into itself. But what a pleasure to keep it alive by

>"Little, nameless, unremembered acts
>Of kindness and of love." [3]

"She whom you loved and chose," says Bondi,

>"Is now your bride,
>The gift of heaven, and to your trust consigned;
>Honor her still, though not with passion blind;
>And in her virtue, though you watch, confide.
>Be to her youth a comfort, guardian, guide,
>　In whose experience she may safety find;
>And whether sweet or bitter be assigned,
>The joy with her, as well as pain divide.

[1] Moore.　　[2] Tennyson.　　[3] Wordsworth.

Yield not too much if reason disapprove;
  Nor too much force; the partner of your life
  Should neither victim be, nor tyrant prove.
Thus shall that rein, which often mars the bliss
  Of wedlock, scarce be felt; and thus your wife
  Ne'er in the husband shall the lover miss." [1]

Every one is ennobled by true love—

  " Tis better to have loved and lost
    Than never to have loved at all." [2]

Perhaps no one ever praised a woman more gracefully in a sentence than Steele when he said of Lady Elizabeth Hastings that " to know her was a liberal education; " but every woman may feel as she improves herself that she is not only laying in a store of happiness for herself, but also raising and blessing him whom she would most wish to see happy and good.

Love, true love, grows and deepens with time. Husband and wife, who are married indeed, live

  " By each other, till to love and live
Be one." [3]

For does it end with life. A mother's love knows no bounds.

  " They err who tell us Love can die,
    With life all other passions fly,
      All others are but vanity.

[1] Bondi. Tr. by Glassfors.
[2] Tennyson.   [3] Swinburne.

In Heaven Ambition cannot dwell,
Nor Avarice in the vaults of Hell;
Earthly these passions of the Earth;
They perish where they have their birth,
   But Love is indestructible;
   Its holy flame forever burneth,
From Heaven it came, to Heaven returneth;
   Too oft on Earth a troubled guest,
   At times deceived, at times opprest,
   It here is tried and purified,
   Then hath in Heaven its perfect rest:
It soweth here with toil and care,
But the harvest time of Love is there.

"The mother when she meets on high
   The Babe she lost in infancy,
Hath she not then, for pains and fears,
   The day of woe, the watchful night,
   For all her sorrow, all her tears,
   An over-payment of delight?"[1]

As life wears on the love of husband or wife, of friends and of children, becomes the great solace and delight of age. The one recalls the past, the other gives interest to the future; and in our children, it has been truly said, we live our lives again.

[1] Southey.

CHAPTER V.

ART.

"High art consists neither in altering, nor in improving nature; but in seeking throughout nature for 'whatsoever things are lovely, whatsoever things are pure;' in loving these, in displaying to the utmost of the painter's power such loveliness as is in them, and directing the thoughts of others to them by winning art, or gentle emphasis. Art (caeteris paribus) is great in exact proportion to the love of beauty shown by the painter, provided that love of beauty forfeit no atom of truth."—RUSKIN.

CHAPTER V.

ART.

THE most ancient works of Art which we possess are representations of animals, rude indeed, but often strikingly characteristic, engraved on, or carved in, stag's-horn or bone; and found in English, French, and German caves, with stone and other rude implements, and the remains of mammalia, belonging apparently to the close of the glacial epoch: not only of the deer, bear, and other animals now inhabiting temperate Europe, but of some, such as the reindeer, the musk sheep, and the mammoth, which have either retreated north or become altogether extinct. We may, I think, venture to hope that other designs may hereafter be found, which will give us additional information as to the manners and customs of our ancestors in those remote ages.

Next to these in point of antiquity come the sculptures and paintings on Assyrian and Egyptian tombs, temples, and palaces.

These ancient scenes, considered as works of art, have no doubt many faults, and yet how graphically they tell their story! As a matter of fact a king is not, as a rule, bigger than his soldiers, but in these battle-scenes he is always so represented. We must, however, remember that in ancient warfare the greater part of the fighting was, as a matter of fact, done by the chiefs. In this respect the Homeric poems resemble the Assyrian and Egyptian representations. At any rate, we see at a glance which is the king, which are officers, which side is victorious, the struggles and sufferings of the wounded, the flight of the enemy, the city of refuge—so that he who runs may read; while in modern battle-pictures the story is much less clear, and, indeed, the untrained eye sees for some time little but scarlet and smoke.

These works assuredly possess a grandeur and dignity of their own, even though they have not the beauty of later art.

In Greece Art reached a perfection which has never been excelled, and it was more appreciated than perhaps it has ever been since.

At the time when Demetrius attacked the city of Rhodes, Protogenes was painting a picture of Ialysus. "This," says Pliny, "hindered King Demetrius from taking Rhodes, out of fear lest he should burn the picture; and not being able to fire the town on any other side, he was pleased rather to spare the painting than to take the victory, which was already in his hands. Protogenes, at that time, had his painting-room in a garden out of the town, and very near the camp of the enemies, where he was daily finishing those pieces which he had already begun, the noise of soldiers not being capable of interrupting his studies. But Demetrius causing him to be brought into his presence, and asking him what made him so bold as to work in the midst of enemies, he answered the king, 'That he understood the war which he made was against the Rhodians, and not against the Arts.'"

With the decay of Greece, Art sank too, until it was revived in the thirteenth century by Cimabue, since whose time its progress has been triumphal.

Art is unquestionably one of the purest and highest elements in human happiness. It trains the mind through the eye, and the eye through the mind. As the sun colors flowers, so does art color life.

"In true Art," says Ruskin, "the hand, the head, and the heart of man go together. But Art is no recreation: it cannot be learned at spare moments, nor pursued when we have nothing better to do."

It is not only in the East that great works, really due to study and labor, have been attributed to magic.

Study and labor cannot make every man an artist, but no one can succeed in art without them. In Art two and two do not make four, and no number of little things will make a great one.

It has been said, and on high authority, that the end of art is to please. But this is a very imperfect definition. It might as well be said that a library is only intended for pleasure and ornament.

Art has the advantage of nature, in so far as it introduces a human element, which is in some respects superior even to nature. "If," says Plato, "you take a man as he is made by nature and compare him with another who is the effect of art, the work of nature will always appear the less beautitiful, because art is more accurate than nature."

Bacon also, in *The Advancement of Learning*, speaks of "the world being inferior to the soul, by reason whereof there is agreeable to the spirit of man a more ample greatness, a more exact goodness, and a more absolute variety than can be found in the nature of things."

The poets tell us that Prometheus, having made a beautiful statue of Minerva, the goddess was so delighted that she offered to bring down anything from Heaven which could add to its perfection. Prometheus on this prudently asked her to take him there, so that he might choose for himself. This Minerva did, and Prometheus, finding that in heaven all things were animated by fire, brought back a spark, with which he gave life to his work.

In fact, Imitation is the means and not the end of Art. The story of Zeuxis and Parrhasius is a pretty tale; but to deceive birds, or even man himself, is but a trifling matter compared with the higher functions of Art. To imitate the *Iliad*, says Dr. Young, is not imitating Homer, but as Sir J. Reynolds adds, the more the artist studies nature "the nearer he approaches to the true and perfect idea of art."

"Following these rules and using these precautions, when you have clearly and distinctly learned in what good coloring consists, you cannot do better than have recourse to Nature herself, who is always at hand, and in comparison of whose true splendor the best colored pictures are but faint and feeble."[1]

Art, indeed, must create as well as copy. As Victor Cousin well says, "The ideal without the real lacks life; but the real without the ideal lacks pure beauty. Both need to unite; to join hands and enter into alliance. In this way the best work may be achieved. Thus beauty is an absolute idea, and not a mere copy of imperfect Nature."

The grouping of the picture is of course of the utmost importance. Sir Joshua Reynolds gives two remarkable cases to show how much any given figure in a picture is affected by its surroundings. Tintoret in one of his pictures has taken the Samson of Michael Angelo, put an eagle under him, placed thunder and lightning in his right hand instead of the jawbone of an ass, and thus turned him into a Jupiter. The second instance is even more striking. Titian has copied the figure in the vault of the Sistine Chapel which represents the Deity dividing light from darkness, and has introduced it into his picture of the battle of Cadore, to represent a general falling from his horse.

[1] Reynolds.

We must remember that so far as the eye is concerned, the object of the artist is to train, not to deceive, and that his higher function has reference rather to the mind than to the eye.

No doubt

> "To gild refined gold, to paint the lily,
> To throw a perfume on the violet,
> To smooth the ice, or add another hue
> Unto the rainbow, or with taper-light
> To seek the beauteous eye of heaven to garnish,
> Is wasteful and ridiculous excess." [1]

But all is not gold that glitters, flowers are not all arrayed like the lily, and there is room for selection as well as representation.

"The true, the good, and the beautiful," says Cousin, "are but forms of the infinite: what then do we really love in truth, beauty, and virtue? We love the infinite himself. The love of the infinite substance is hidden under the love of its forms. It is so truly the infinite which charms in the true, the good, and the beautiful, that its manifestations alone do not suffice. The artist is dissatisfied at the sight even of his greatest works; he aspires still higher."

It is indeed sometimes objected that Landscape painting is not true to nature; but we must ask, What is truth? Is the object to produce the same impression on the mind as that created by the scene itself? If so, let any one try to draw from

[1] Shakespeare.

memory a group of mountains, and he will probably find that in the impression produced on his mind the mountains are loftier and steeper, the valleys deeper and narrower, than in the actual reality. A drawing, then, which was literally exact would not be true, in the sense of conveying the same impression as Nature herself.

In fact, Art, says Goethe, is called Art simply because it is not Nature.

It is not sufficient for the artist to choose beautiful scenery, and delineate it with accuracy. He must not be a mere copyist. Something higher and more subtle is required. He must create, or at any rate interpret, as well as copy.

Turner was never satisfied merely to reach to even the most glorious scenery. He moved, and even suppressed, mountains.

A certain nobleman, we are told, was very anxious to see the model from whom Guido painted his lovely female faces. Guido placed his color-grinder, a big coarse man, in an attitude, and then drew a beautiful Magdalen. "My dear Count," he said, "the beautiful and pure idea must be in the mind, and then it is no matter what the model is."

Guido Reni, who painted St. Michael for the Church of the Capuchins at Rome, wished that he "had the wings of an angel, to have ascended unto Paradise, and there to have beheld the forms of those beautiful spirits, from which I might have copied my Archangel. But not being able to mount so high, it was in vain for me to seek for his resemblance here below; so that I was forced to look into mine own mind, and into that idea of beauty which I have formed in my own imagination." [1]

Science attempts, as far as the limited powers of Man permit, to reproduce the actual facts in a manner which, however bald, is true in itself, irrespective of time and scene. To do this she must submit to many limitations; not altogether unvexatious, and not without serious drawbacks. Art, on the contrary, endeavors to convey the impression of the original under some especial aspect.

In some respects, Art gives a clearer and more vivid idea of an unknown country than any description can convey. In literature rock may be rock, but in painting it must be granite or slate, and not merely rock in general.

It is remarkable that while artists have long recognized the necessity of studying anatomy, and there has been from the commencement a professor of anatomy in the Royal Academy, it is only of late years that any knowledge of botany or geology has been considered desirable, and even now their importance is by no means generally recognized.

Much has been written as to the relative merits of painting, sculpture, and architecture. This, if it be not a somewhat unprofitable inquiry, would at any rate be out of place here.

Architecture not only gives intense pleasure, but

[1] Dryden.

even the impression of something ethereal and superhuman.

Madame de Staël described it as "frozen music;" and a cathedral is a glorious specimen of "thought in stone," whose very windows are transparent walls of gorgeous hues.

Caracci said that poets paint in their words and artists speak in their works. The latter have indeed one great advantage, for a glance at a statue or a painting will convey a more vivid idea than a long and minute description.

Another advantage possessed by Art is that it is understood by all civilized nations, whilst each has a separate language.

Even from a material point of view Art is most important. In a recent address Sir F. Leighton has observed that the study of Art "is every day becoming more important in relation to certain sides of the waning material prosperity of the country. For the industrial competition between this and other countries—a competition, keen and eager, which means to certain industries almost a race for life—runs, in many cases, no longer exclusively or mainly on the lines of excellence of material and solidity of workmanship, but greatly nowadays on the lines of artistic charm and beauty of design."

The highest service, however, that Art can accomplish for man is to become " at once the voice of his nobler aspirations, and the steady disciplinarian of his emotions; and it is with this mission, rather than with any æsthetic perfection, that we are at present concerned."[1]

Science and Art are sisters, or rather perhaps they are like brother and sister. The mission of Art is in some respects like that of woman. It is not Hers so much to do the hard toil and moil of the world, as to surround it with a halo of beauty, to convert work into pleasure.

In science we naturally expect progress, but in Art the case is not so clear; and yet Sir Joshua Reynolds did not hesitate to express his conviction that in the future " so much will painting improve, that the best we can now achieve will appear like the work of children," and we may hope that our power of enjoying it may increase in an equal ratio. Wordsworth says that poets have to create the taste for their own works, and the same is, in some degree at any rate, true of artists.

In one respect especially modern painters appear to have made a marked advance, and one great blessing which in fact we owe to them is a more vivid enjoyment of scenery.

I have of course no pretensions to speak with authority, but even in the case of the greatest masters before Turner, the landscapes seem to me singularly inferior to the figures. Sir Joshua Reynolds tells us that Gainsborough framed a kind of model of a landscape on his table, composed of broken stones, dried herbs, and pieces of looking-glass, which he magnified and improved into rocks,

[1] Haweis.

trees, and water; and Sir Joshua solemnly discusses the wisdom of such a proceeding. "How far it may be useful in giving hints," he says, "the professors of landscape can best determine," but he does not recommend it, and is disposed to think, on the whole, the practice may be more likely to do harm than good!

In the picture of Ceyx and Alcyone, by Wilson, of whom Cunningham said that, with Gainsborough, he laid the foundation of our School of Landscape, the castle is said to have been painted from a pot of porter, and the rock from a Stilton cheese. There is indeed another version of the story, that the picture was sold for a pot of porter and a cheese, which, however, does not give a higher idea of the appreciation of the art of landscape at that date.

Until very recently the general feeling with reference to mountain scenery has been that expressed by Tacitus. "Who would leave Asia or Africa or Italy to go to Germany, a shapeless and unformed country, a harsh sky, and melancholy aspect, unless indeed it was his native land?"

It is amusing to read the opinion of Dr. Beattie, in a special treatise on *Truth, Poetry and Music*, written at the close of the last century, that "The Highlands of Scotland are in general a melancholy country. Long tracts of mountainous country, covered with dark heath, and often obscured by misty weather; narrow valleys thinly inhabited, and bounded by precipices resounding with the fall of torrents; a soil so rugged, and a climate so dreary, as in many parts to admit neither the amenities of pasturage, nor the labors of agriculture; the mournful dashing of waves along the firths and lakes; the portentous noises which every change of the wind is apt to raise in a lonely region, full of echoes, and rocks, and caverns; the grotesque and ghastly appearance of such a landscape by the light of the moon: objects like these diffuse a gloom over the fancy," etc.[1]

Even Goldsmith regarded the scenery of the Highlands as dismal and hideous. Johnson, we know, laid it down as an axiom that "the noblest prospect which a Scotchman ever sees is the high road that leads him to England"—a saying which throws much doubt on his distinction that the Giant's Causeway was "worth seeing but not worth going to see."[2]

Madame de Staël declared, that though she would go 500 leagues to meet a clever man, she would not care to open her window to see the Bay of Naples.

Nor was the ancient absence of appreciation confined to scenery. Even Burke, speaking of Stonehenge, says, "Stonehenge, neither for disposition nor ornament, has anything admirable."

Ugly scenery, however, may in some cases have an injurious effect on the human system. It has been ingeniously suggested that what really drove Don Quixote out of his mind was not the

[1] Beattie, 1776. [2] Boswell.

study of his books of chivalry, so much as the monotonous scenery of La Mancha.

The love of landscape is not indeed due to Art alone. It has been the happy combination of art and science which has trained us to perceive the beauty which surrounds us.

Art helps us to see, and "hundreds of people can talk for one who can think; but thousands can think for one who can see. To see clearly is poetry, prophecy, and religion all in one. . . . Remembering always that there are two characters in which all greatness of Art consists—first, the earnest and intense seizing of natural facts; then the ordering those facts by strength of human intellect, so as to make them, for all who look upon them, to the utmost serviceable, memorable, and beautiful. And thus great Art is nothing else than the type of strong and noble life; for as the ignoble person, in his dealings with all that occurs in the world about him, first sees nothing clearly, looks nothing fairly in the face, and then allows himself to be swept away by the trampling torrent and unescapable force of the things that he would not foresee and could not understand: so the noble person, looking the facts of the world full in the face, and fathoming them with deep faculty, then deals with them in unalarmed intelligence and unhurried strength, and becomes, with his human intellect and will, no unconscious nor insignificant agent in consummating their good and restraining their evil." [1]

[1] Ruskin.

May we not also hope that in this respect also still further progress may be made, that beauties may be revealed, and pleasures may be in store for those who come after us, which we cannot appreciate, or at least can but faintly feel.

Even now there is scarcely a cottage without something more or less successfully claiming to rank as Art,—a picture, a photograph, or a statu, ette; and we may fairly hope that much as Art even now contributes to the happiness of life, it will do so even more effectively in the future.

CHAPTER VI.

POETRY.

"And here the singer for his Art
 Not all in vain may plead;
The song that nerves a nation's heart
 Is in itself a deed."

TENNYSON.

CHAPTER VI.

POETRY.

AFTER the disastrous defeat of the Athenians before Syracuse, Plutarch tells us that the Sicilians spared those who could repeat any of the poetry of Euripides.

"Some there were," he says, "who owed their preservation to Euripides. Of all the Grecians, his was the muse with whom the Sicilians were most in love. From the strangers who landed in their island they gleaned every small specimen or portion of his works, and communicated it with pleasure to each other. It is said that upon this occasion a number of Athenians on their return home went to Euripides, and thanked him in the most grateful manner for their obligations to his pen; some having been enfranchised for teaching their masters what they remembered of his poems, and others having procured refreshments, when they were wandering about after the battle, by singing a few of his verses."

Nowadays we are none of us likely to owe our lives to Poetry in this sense, yet in another we many of us owe to it a similar debt. How often, when worn with overwork, sorrow, or anxiety, have we taken down Homer or Horace, Shakespeare or Milton, and felt the clouds gradually roll away, the jar of nerves subside, the consciousness of power replace physical exhaustion, and the darkness of despondency brighten once more into the light of life.

"And yet Plato," says Jowett, "expels the poets from his Republic because they are allied to sense; because they stimulate the emotions; because they are thrice removed from the ideal truth."

In that respect, as in some others, few would accept Plato's Republic as being an ideal Commonwealth, and most would agree with Sir Philip Sidney that "if you cannot bear the planet-like music of poetry . . . I must send you in the behalf of all poets, that while you live, you live in love, and never get favor for lacking skill of a sonnet; and when you die, your memory die from the earth, for want of an epitaph."

Poetry has often been compared with painting and sculpture. Simonides long ago said that Poetry is a speaking picture, and painting is mute Poetry.

"Poetry," says Cousin, "is the first of the Arts because it best represents the infinite."

And again, "Though the arts are in some respects isolated, yet there is one which seems to profit by the resources of all, and that is Poetry. With words, Poetry can paint and sculpture; she can build edifices like an architect; she unites, to some extent, melody and music. She is, so to say, the center in which all arts unite."

A true poem is a gallery of pictures.

It must, I think, be admitted that painting and sculpture can give us a clearer and more vivid idea of an object we have never seen than any description can convey. But when we have once seen it, then on the contrary there are many points which the poet brings before us, and which perhaps neither in the representation, nor even in nature, should we perceive for ourselves. Objects can be most vividly brought before us by the artist, actions by the poet; space is the domain of Art, time of Poetry.[1]

Take, for instance, as a typical instance, female beauty. How labored and how cold any description appears. The greatest poets recognize this; as, for instance, when Scott wishes us to realize the Lady of the Lake he does not attempt any description, but just mentions her attitude and then adds—

> "And ne'er did Grecian chisel trace
> A Nymph, a Naiad, or a Grace,
> Of finer form or lovelier face!"

A great poet indeed must be inspired; he must possess an exquisite sense of beauty, and feelings deeper than those of most men, and yet well under his control. "The Milton of poetry is the man,

[1] See Lessing's *Luocoön*.

in his own magnificent phrase, of devout prayer to that eternal spirit that can enrich with all utterance and knowledge, and sends out his seraphim with the hallowed fire of his altar, to touch and purify the lips of whom he pleases." [1] And if from one point of view Poetry brings home to us the immeasurable inequalities of different minds, on the other hand it teaches us that genius is no affair of rank or wealth.

> "I think of Chatterton, the marvellous boy,
> The sleepless soul, that perish'd in his pride;
> Of Burns, that walk'd in glory and in joy
> Behind his plough upon the mountain-side." [2]

A man may be a poet and yet write no verse, but not if he writes bad or poor ones.

> "Mediocribus esse poetis
> Non homines, non Di, non concessere columnæ." [3]

Second-rate poets, like second-rate writers generally, fade gradually into dreamland; but the great poets remain always.

Poetry will not live unless it be alive, "that which comes from the head goes to the heart;" [4] and Milton truly said that "he who would not be frustrate of his hope to write well hereafter in laudable things, ought himself to be a true poem."

For "he who, having no touch of the Muses' madness in his soul, comes to the door and thinks

[1] Arnold. [2] Coleridge. [3] Horace. [4] Wordsworth.

he will get into the temple by the help of Art—he, I say, and his Poetry are not admitted."[1]

But the work of the true poet is immortal.

" For have not the verses of Homer continued 2500 years or more without the loss of a syllable or a letter, during which time infinite palaces, temples, castles, cities, have been decayed and demolished? It is not possible to have the true pictures or statues of Cyrus, Alexander, Cæsar, no, nor of the kings or great personages of much later years; for the originals cannot last, and the copies cannot but lose of the life and truth. But the images of men's wits and knowledge remain in books, exempted from the wrong of time and capable of perpetual renovation. Neither are they fitly to be called images, because they generate still and cast their seeds in the minds of others, provoking and causing infinite actions and opinions in succeeding ages: so that if the invention of the ship was thought so noble, which carrieth riches and commodities from place to place, and consociateth the most remote regions in participation of their fruits, how much more are letters to be magnified, which, as ships, pass through the vast seas of time and make ages so distant to participate of the wisdom, illuminations, and inventions, the one of the other?"[2]

The poet requires many qualifications. "Who has traced," says Cousin, "the plan of this poem? Reason. Who has given it life and charm? Love.

[1] Plato. [2] Bacon.

And who has guided reason and love? The Will."

> "All men have some imagination, but
> The Lover and the Poet
> Are of imagination all compact.
>
> . . . . .
>
> The Poet's eye, in a fine frenzy rolling,
> Doth glance from heaven to earth, from earth to heaven,
> And as imagination bodies forth
> The forms of things unknown, the poet's pen
> Turns them to shapes, and gives to airy nothing
> A local habitation and a name." [1]

Poetry is the fruit of genius; but it cannot be produced without labor. Moore, one of the airiest of poets, tells us that he was a slow and painstaking workman.

The works of our greatest Poets are all episodes in that one great poem which the geuius of man has created since the commencement of human history.

A distinguished mathematician is said once to have inquired what was proved by Milton in his *Paradise Lost;* and there are no doubt still some who ask themselves, even if they shrink from putting the question to others, whether Poetry is of any use, just as if to give pleasure were not useful in itself. No true Utilitarian, however, would feel this doubt, since the greatest happiness of the greatest number is the rule of his philosophy.

[1] Shakespeare.

"We must not estimate the works of genius merely with reference to the pleasure they afford, even when pleasure was their principal object. We must also regard the intelligence which they presuppose and exercise."[1]

Thoroughly to enjoy Poetry we must not so limit ourselves, but must rise to a higher ideal.

"Yes; constantly in reading poetry, a sense for the best, the really excellent, and of the strength and joy to be drawn from it, should be present in our minds, and should govern our estimate of what we read."[2]

Cicero, in his oration for Archias, well asked, "Has not this man then a right to my love, to my admiration, to all the means which I can employ in his defence? For we are instructed by all the greatest and most learned of mankind, that education, precepts, and practice, can in every other branch of learning produce excellence. But a poet is formed by the hand of nature; he is aroused by mental vigor, and inspired by what we may call the spirit of divinity itself. Therefore our Ennius has a right to give to poets the epithet of Holy,[3] because they are, as it were, lent to mankind by the indulgent bounty of the gods."

"Poetry," says Shelley, "awakens and enlarges the mind itself by rendering it the receptacle of a thousand unapprehended combinations of thought. Poetry lifts the veil from the hidden beauty of the

[1] St. Hilaire.   [2] Arnold.
[3] Plato styles poets the sons and interpreters of the gods.

world, and makes familiar objects be as if they were not familiar; it reproduces all that it represents, and the impersonations clothed in its Elysian light stand thenceforward in the minds of those who have once contemplated them, as memorials of that gentle and exalted content which extends itself over all thoughts and actions with which it co-exists."

And again, "All high Poetry is infinite; it is as the first acorn, which contained all oaks potentially. Veil after veil may be undrawn, and the inmost naked beauty of the meaning never exposed. A great poem is a fountain forever overflowing with the waters of wisdom and delight."

Or, as he has expressed himself in his Ode to a Skylark:

> "Higher still and higher
> From the earth thou springest
> Like a cloud of fire;
> The blue deep thou wingest,
> And singing still dost soar, and soaring ever singest.
>
> "Like a poet hidden
> In the light of thought,
> Singing hymns unbidden,
> Till the world is wrought
> To sympathy with hopes and fears it heeded not.
>
> "Like a glow-worm golden
> In a dell of dew,
> Scattering unbeholden
> Its aërial hue
> Among the flowers and grass, which screen it from the view."

We speak now of the poet as the Maker or Creator—ποιητής; the origin of the word "bard" seems doubtful.

The Hebrews well called their poets "Seers," for they not only perceive more than others, but also help other men to see much which would otherwise be lost to us. The old Greek word was ἀοιδός—the Bard or Singer.

Poetry lifts the veil from the beauty of the world which would otherwise be hidden, and throws over the most familiar objects the glow and halo of imagination. The man who has a love for Poetry can scarcely fail to derive intense pleasure from Nature, which to those who love it is all "beauty to the eye and music to the ear."

"Yet Nature never set forth the earth in so rich tapestry as divers poets have done; neither with so pleasant rivers, fruitful trees, sweet-smelling flowers, nor whatsoever else may make the too-much-loved earth more lovely."[1]

In the smokiest city the poet will transport us, as if by enchantment, to the fresh air and bright sun, to the murmur of woods and leaves and water, to the ripple of waves upon sand, and enable us, as in some delightful dream, to cast off the cares and troubles of life.

The poet, indeed, must have more true knowledge, not only of human nature, but of all Nature, than other men are gifted with.

Crabbe Robinson tells us that when a stranger

[1] Sydney, *Defence of Poetry.*

once asked permission to see Wordsworth's study, the maid said, "This is master's Library, but he studies in the fields." No wonder then that Nature has been said to return the poet's love.

> "Call it not vain;—they do not err
> Who say that, when the poet dies,
> Mute Nature mourns her worshipper,
> And celebrates his obsequies."[1]

Swinburne says of Blake, and I feel entirely with him, though in my case the application would have been different, that "The sweetness of sky and leaf, of grass and water—the bright light life of bird, child, and beast—is, so to speak, kept fresh by some graver sense of faithful and mysterious love, explained and vivified by a conscience and purpose in the artist's hand and mind. Such a fiery outbreak of spring, such an insurrection of fierce floral life and radiant riot of childish power and pleasure, no poet or painter ever gave before; such lustre of green leaves and flushed limbs, kindled cloud and fervent fleece, was never wrought into speech or shape."

To appreciate Poetry we must not merely glance at it, or rush through it, or read it in order to talk or write about it. One must compose oneself into the right frame of mind. Of course for one's own sake one will read Poetry in times of agitation, sorrow, or anxiety, but that is another matter.

[1] Scott.

The inestimable treasures of Poetry again are open to all of us. The best books are indeed the cheapest. For the price of a little beer, a little tobacco, we can buy Shakespeare or Milton—or indeed almost as many books as a man can read with profit in a year.

Nor, in considering the advantage of Poetry to man, must we limit ourselves to its past or present influence. The future of Poetry, says Mr. Matthew Arnold, and no one was more qualified to speak, " The future of Poetry is immense, because in Poetry, where it is worthy of its high destinies, our race, as time goes on, will find an ever surer and surer stay. But for Poetry the idea is everything; the rest is a world of illusion, of divine illusion. Poetry attaches its emotion to the idea; the idea *is* the fact. The strongest part of our religion to-day is its unconscious Poetry. We should conceive of Poetry worthily, and more highly than it has been the custom to conceive of it. We should conceive of it as capable of higher uses, and called to higher destinies than those which in general men have assigned to it hitherto."

Poetry has been well called the record " of the best and happiest moments of the happiest and best minds; " it is the light of life, the very " image of life expressed in its eternal truth ; " it immortalizes all that is best and most beautiful in the world ; " it purges from our inward sight the film of familiarity which obscures from us the wonder of our being ; " " it is the center and circumference of knowledge ; " and poets are " mirrors of the gigantic shadows which futurity casts upon the present."

Poetry, in effect, lengthens life; it creates for us time, if time be realized as the succession of ideas and not of minutes; it is the " breath and finer spirit of all knowledge ; " it is bound neither by time nor space, but lives in the spirit of man. What greater praise can be given than the saying that life should be Poetry put into action.

CHAPTER VII.

MUSIC.

"Music is a moral law. It gives a soul to the universe, wings to the mind, flight to the imagination, a charm to sadness, gaiety and life to everything. It is the essence of order, and leads to all that is good, just, and beautiful, of which it is the invisible, but nevertheless dazzling, passionate, and eternal form."—PLATO.

CHAPTER VII.

MUSIC.

MUSIC is in one sense far more ancient than man, and the voice was from the very commencement of human existence a source of melody: but so far as musical instruments are concerned, it is probable that percussion came first, then wind instruments, and lastly, those with strings: first the Drum, then the Flute, and thirdly, the Lyre. The early history of Music is, however, unfortunately wrapped in much obscurity. The use of letters long preceded the invention of notes, and tradition in such a matter can tell us but little.

The contest between Marsyas and Apollo is supposed by some to typify the struggle between the Flute and the Lyre; Marsyas representing the archaic Flute, Apollo the champion of the Lyre. The latter of course was victorious: it sets the voice free, and the sound

> "Of music that is born of human breath
> Comes straighter to the soul than any strain
> The hand alone can make."[1]

[1] Morris.

Various myths have grown up to explain the origin of Music. One Greek tradition was to the effect Grasshoppers were human beings themselves in a world before the Muses; that when the Muses came, being ravished with delight, they sang and sang and forgot to eat, until "they died of hunger for the love of song. And they carry to heaven the report of those who honor them on earth."[1]

The old writers and commentators tell us that Pythagoras, "as he was one day meditating on the want of some rule to guide the ear, analogous to what had been used to help the other senses, chanced to pass by a blacksmith's shop, and observing that the hammers, which were four in number, sounded very harmoniously, he had them weighed, and found them to be in the proportion of six, eight, nine, and twelve. Upon this he suspended four strings of equal length and thickness, etc., fastened weights in the above-mentioned proportions to each of them respectively, and found that they gave the same sounds that the hammers had done; viz. the fourth, fifth, and octave to the gravest tone."[2] However this may be, it would appear that the lyre had at first four strings only; Terpander is said to have given it three more, and an eighth was subsequently added.

We have unfortunately no specimens of Greek or Roman, or even of Early Christian music. The Chinese indicated the notes by words or their initials. The lowest was termed "Koung," or the

[1] Plato. [2] Crowest.

Emperor, as being the Foundation on which all were supported; the second was Tschang, the Prime Minister; the third, the Subject; the fourth, Public Business; the fifth, the Mirror of Heaven.[1] The Greeks also had a name for each note. The so-called Gregorian notes were not invented until six hundred years after Gregory's death. The Monastery of St. Gall possesses a copy of Gregory's Antiphonary, made about the year 780 by a chorister who was sent from Rome to Charlemagne to reform the Northern music, and in this the notes are indicated by "pneumss," from which our notes were gradually developed, and first arranged along one line, to which others were gradually added. But I must not enlarge on this interesting subject.

In the matter of music Englishmen have certainly deserved well of the world. Even as long ago as 1185 Giraldus Cambrensis, Bishop of St. David's, says, "The Britons do not sing their tunes in unison like the inhabitants of other countries, but in different parts. So that when a company of singers meet to sing, as is usual in this country, as many different parts are heard as there are singers."[2]

The most ancient known piece of music for several voices is an English four men's song, "Summer is a-coming in," which is considered to be at least as early as 1240, and is now in the British Museum.

The Venetian Ambassador in the time of Henry

[1] Rowbotham, *History of Music.*   [2] Wakefield.

VIII. said of our English Church music: "The mass was sung by His Majesty's choristers, whose voices are more heavenly than human; they did not chant like men, but like angels."

Speaking of Purcell's anthem, "Be merciful to me, O God," Burney says it is "throughout admirable. Indeed, to my conception there is no better music existing of the kind than the opening of this anthem, in which the verse 'I will praise God' and the last movement in C natural are, in melody, harmony, and modulation, truly divine music."

Dr. Burney says that Purcell was "as much the pride of an Englishman in music as Shakespeare in productions of the stage, Milton in epic poetry, Locke in metaphysics, or Sir Isaac Newton in philosophy and mathematics;" and yet Purcell's music is unfortunately but little known to us now, as Macfarren says, "to our great loss."

The authors of some of the loveliest music, and even in some cases that of comparatively recent times, are unknown to us. This is the case for instance with the exquisite song "Drink to me only with thine eyes," the words of which were taken by Jonson from Philostratus, and which has been considered as the most beautiful of all "people's songs."

The music of "God save the Queen" has been adopted in more than half a dozen other countries, and yet the authorship is a matter of doubt, being attributed by some to Dr. John Bull, by others to

Carey. It was apparently first sung in a tavern in Cornhill.

Both the music and words of "O Death, rock me to sleep" are said to be by Anne Boleyn: "Stay, Corydon" and "Sweet Honey-sucking Bees" by Wildye, "the first of madrigal writers." "Rule Britannia" was composed by Arne, and originally formed part of his Masque of *Alfred*, first performed in 1740 at Cliefden, near Maidenhead. To Arne we are also indebted for the music of "Where the Bee sucks there lurk I." "The Vicar of Bray" is set to a tune originally known as "A Country Garden." "Come unto these yellow sands" we owe to Purcell; "Sigh no more, Ladies" to Stevens; "Home, Sweet Home" to Bishop.

There is a curious melancholy in national music which is generally in the minor key; indeed this holds good with the music of savage races generally. They appear, moreover, to have no love songs.

Herodotus tells us that during the whole time he was in Egypt he only heard one song, and that was a sad one. My own experience there was the same. Some tendency to melancholy seems indeed inherent in music, and Jessica is not alone in the feeling

"I am never merry when I hear sweet music."

The epitaphs on Musicians have been in some

cases very well expressed. Such, for instance, is the following:

> "Philips, whose touch harmonious could remove
> The pangs of guilty power and hapless love,
> Rest here, distressed by poverty no more;
> Here find that calm thou gav'st so oft before;
> Sleep, undisturbed, within this peaceful shrine,
> Till angels wake thee with a note like thine!"

Still more so that on Purcell, whose premature death was so irreparable a loss to English music—

"Here lies Henry Purcell, who left this life, and is gone to that blessed place, where only his harmony can be exceeded."

The histories of Music contain many curious anecdotes as to the circumstances under which different works have been composed.

Rossini tells us that he wrote the overture to the "Gazza Ladra" on the very day of the first performance, in the upper loft of the La Scala, where he had been confined by the manager under the guard of four scene-shifters, who threw the text out of the window to copyists bit by bit as it was composed. Tartini is said to have composed "Il trillo del Diavolo," considered to be his best work, in a dream. Rossini, speaking of the chorus in G minor in his "Dal tuo stellato soglio," tells us: "While I was writing the chorus in G minor I suddenly dipped my pen into a medicine bottle instead of the ink. I made a blot, and when I dried this with the sand it took the form of a natural, which instantly gave me the idea of the effect the change from G minor to G major would make, and to this blot is all the effect, if any, due." But these of course are exceptional cases.

There are other forms of Music, which though not strictly entitled to the name, are yet capable of giving intense pleasure. To the sportsman what Music can excel that of the hounds themselves. The cawing of rooks has been often quoted as a sound which has no actual beauty of its own, and yet which is delightful from its associations.

There is, however, a true Music of Nature,— the song of birds, the whisper of leaves, the ripple of waters upon a sandy shore, the wail of wind or sea.

There was also an ancient impression that the Heavenly bodies give out music as well as light: the Music of the Spheres is proverbial.

> "There's not the smallest orb which thou beholdest
> But in his motion like an angel sings,
> Still quiring to the young-eyed cherubims;
> Such harmony is in immortal souls
> But while this muddy vesture of decay
> Doth grossly close it in, we cannot hear it." [1]

Music indeed often seems as if it scarcely belonged to this material universe, but was

> "A tone
> Of some world far from ours,
> Where music, and moonlight, and feeling are one." [2]

[1] Shakespeare. [2] Swinburne.

There is Music in speech as well as in song. Not merely in the voice of those we love, and the charm of association, but in actual melody; as Milton says,

> "The Angel ended, and in Adam's ear
> So charming left his voice, that he awhile
> Thought him still speaking, still stood fixed to hear."

It is remarkable that more pains are not taken with the voice in conversation as well as in singing, for

> "What plea so tainted and corrupt
> But, being seasoned with a gracious voice,
> Obscures the show of evil."

It may be true as a general rule that

> "The man that hath no Music in himself
> Nor is not moved with concord of sweet sounds
> Is fit for treasons, stratagems, and spoils;"[1]

but there are some notable exceptions. Dr. Johnson had no love of music. On one occasion, hearing that a certain piece of music was very difficult, he expressed his regret that it was not impossible.

Poets, as might have been expected, have sung most sweetly in praise of song. They have, moreover, done so from the most opposite points of view.

[1] Shakespeare.

Milton invokes it as a luxury—

> "And ever against eating cares
> Lap me in soft Lydian airs;
> Married to immortal verse
> Such as the meeting soul may pierce,
> In notes with many a winding bout
> Of linked sweetness long drawn out;
> With wanton heed, and giddy cunning,
> The melting voice through mazes running;
> Untwisting all the chains that tie
> The hidden soul of harmony."

Sometimes as a temptation; so Spenser says of Phædria,

> "And she, more sweet than any bird on bough
> Would oftentimes amongst them bear a part,
> And strive to passe (as she could well enough)
> Their native musicke by her skilful art."

Or as an element of pure happiness—

> "There is in souls a sympathy with sounds;
> And as the mind is pitched, the ear is pleased
> With melting airs or martial, brisk or grave;
> Some chord in unison with what we hear
> Is touched within us, and the heart replies.
> How soft the music of those village bells,
> Falling at intervals upon the ear
> In cadence sweet, now dying all away,
> Now pealing loud again and louder still
> Clear and sonorous, as the gale comes on." [1]

[1] Cowper.

As touching the human heart—

> "The soul of music slumbers in the shell,
> Till waked and kindled by the master's spell,
> And feeling hearts—touch them but lightly—pour
> A thousand melodies unheard before." [1]

As an education—

> "I have sent books and music there, and all
> Those instruments with which high spirits call
> The future from its cradle, and the past
> Out of its grave, and make the present last
> In thoughts and joys which sleep, but cannot die,
> Folded within their own eternity." [2]

As an aid to religion—

> "As from the power of sacred lays
>   The spheres began to move,
> And sung the great Creator's praise
>   To all the blessed above,
> So when the last and dreadful hour
> This crumbling pageant shall devour,
> The trumpet shall be heard on high,
> The dead shall live, the living die,
> And music shall untune the sky." [3]

Or again—

> "Hark how it falls! and now it steals along,
>   Like distant bells upon the lake at eve,
> When all is still; and now it grows more strong
>   As when the choral train their dirges weave

[1] Rogers. [2] Shelley. [3] Dryden.

> Mellow and many voiced; where every close
>   O'er the old minster roof, in echoing waves reflows.
> Oh! I am rapt aloft. My spirit soars
>   Beyond the skies, and leaves the stars behind;
> Lo! angels lead me to the happy shores,
>   And floating pæans fill the buoyant wind.
> Farewell! base earth, farewell! my soul is freed."

The power of Music to sway the feelings of Man has never been more cleverly portrayed than by Dryden in "The Feast of Alexander," though the circumstances of the case precluded any reference to the influence of Music in its noblest aspects.

Poets have always attributed to Music—and who would wish to deny it?—a power even over the inanimate forces of Nature. Shakespeare accounts for shooting stars by the attraction of Music:

> "The rude sea grew civil at her song,
>   And certain stars shot madly from their spheres
>   To hear the Sea-maid's music."

Prose writers have also been inspired by Music to their highest eloquence. "Music," says Plato, "is a moral law. It gives a soul to the universe, wings to the mind, flight to the imagination, a charm to sadness, gaiety and life to everything. It is the essence of order, and leads to all that is good, just, and beautiful, of which it is the invisible, but nevertheless dazzling, passionate, and eternal form." "Music," said Luther, "is a fair and glorious gift from God. I would not for the world renounce my humble share in music." "Music," said Halevy, " is an art that God has given us, in which the voices of all nations may unite their prayers in one harmonious rhythm." Or Carlyle, "Music is a kind of inarticulate, unfathomable speech, which leads us to the edge of the infinite, and lets us for moments gaze into it."

Let me also quote Helmholtz, one of the profoundest exponents of modern science. "Just as in the rolling ocean, this movement, rhythmically repeated, and yet ever-varying, rivets our attention and hurries us along. But whereas in the sea blind physical forces alone are at work, and hence the final impression on the spectator's mind is nothing but solitude—in a musical work of art the movement follows the outflow of the artist's own emotions. Now gently gliding, now gracefully leaping, now violently stirred, penetrated, or laboriously contending with the natural expression of passion, the stream of sound, in primitive vivacity, bears over into the hearer's soul unimagined moods which the artist has overheard from his own, and finally raises him up to that repose of everlasting beauty of which God has allowed but few of his elect favorites to be the heralds."

"There are but seven notes in the scale; make them fourteen," says Newman, "yet what a slender outfit for so vast an enterprise! What science brings so much out of so little? Out of what poor elements does some great master in it create his new world! Shall we say that all this exuberant inventiveness is a mere ingenuity or trick of art, like some game of fashion of the day, without reality, without meaning? . . . Is it possible that that inexhaustible evolution and disposition of notes, so rich yet so simple, so intricate yet so regulated, so various yet so majestic, should be a mere sound, which is gone and perishes? Can it be that those mysterious stirrings of the heart, and keen emotions, and strange yearnings after we know not what, and awful impressions from we know not whence, should be wrought in us by what is unsubstantial, and comes and goes, and begins and ends in itself? it is not so; it cannot be. No; they have escaped from some higher sphere; they are the outpourings of eternal harmony in the medium of created sound; they are echoes from our Home; they are the voices of Angels, or the Magnificat of Saints, or the living laws of Divine Governance, or the Divine Attributes; something are they besides themselves, which we cannot compass, which we cannot utter, though mortal man, and he perhaps not otherwise distinguished above his fellows, has the gift of eliciting them."

Poetry and Music unite in song. From the earliest ages song has been the sweet companion of labor. The rude chant of the boatman floats upon the water, the shepherd sings upon the hill, the milkmaid in the dairy, the ploughman at the plough. Every trade, every occupation, every act and scene of life, has long had its own especial music. The bride went to her marriage, the laborer to his work, the old man to his last long rest, each with appropriate and immemorial music.

Music has been truly described as the mother of sympathy, the handmaid of Religion, and will never exercise its full effect, as the Emperor Charles VI. said to Farinelli, unless it aims not merely to charm the ear, but to touch the heart.

There are many who consider that our life at present is peculiarly prosaic and mercenary. I greatly doubt whether that be the case, but if so our need for Music is all the more imperative.

Much as Music has already done for man, we may hope even more from it in the future.

It is, moreover, a joy for all. To appreciate Science or Art requires some training, and no doubt the cultivated ear will more and more appreciate the beauties of Music; but though there are exceptional individuals, and even races, almost devoid of any love of Music, still they are happily but rare.

Good Music, moreover, does not necessarily involve any considerable outlay; it is even now no mere luxury of the rich, and we may hope that as time goes on, it will become more and more the comfort and solace of the poor.

CHAPTER VIII.

THE BEAUTIES OF NATURE.

"Speak to the earth and it shall teach thee."
                                    JOB.

"And this our life, exempt from public haunt,
   Finds tongues in trees, books in the running brooks,
   Sermons in stones, and good in everything."
                                    SHAKESPEARE.

CHAPTER VIII.

THE BEAUTIES OF NATURE.

WE are told in the first chapter of Genesis that at the close of the sixth day "God saw every thing that he had made, and, behold, it was very good." Not merely good, but very good. Yet how few of us appreciate the beautiful world in which we live!

In preceding chapters I have incidentally, though only incidentally, referred to the Beauties of Nature; but any attempt, however imperfect, to sketch the blessings of life must contain some special reference to this lovely world itself, which the Greeks happily called κόσμος—beauty.

Hamerton, in his charming work on *Landscape*, says, "There are, I believe, four new experiences for which no description ever adequately prepares us, the first sight of the sea, the first journey in the desert, the sight of flowing molten lava, and a walk on a great glacier. We feel in each case that the strange thing is pure nature, as much nature as a familiar English moor, yet so extraordinary that we might be in another planet." But it would, I think, be easier to enumerate the Wonders of

Nature for which description can prepare us, than those which are altogether beyond the power of language.

Many of us, however, walk through the world like ghosts, as if we were in it, but not of it. We have "eyes and see not, ears and hear not." To look is much less easy than to overlook, and to be able to see what we do see, is a great gift. Ruskin maintains that "The greatest thing a human soul ever does in this world is to see something, and tell what it saw in a plain way." I do not suppose that his eyes are better than ours, but how much more he sees with them!

We must look before we can expect to see. "To the attentive eye," says Emerson, "each moment of the year has its own beauty; and in the same field it beholds every hour a picture that was never seen before, and shall never be seen again. The heavens change every moment and reflect their glory or gloom on the plains beneath."

The love of Nature is a great gift, and if it is frozen or crushed out, the character can hardly fail to suffer from the loss. I will not, indeed, say that a person who does not love Nature is necessarily bad; or that one who does, is necessarily good; but it is to most minds a great help. Many, as Miss Cobbe says, enter the Temple through the gate called Beautiful.

There are doubtless some to whom none of the beautiful wonders of Nature; neither the glories of the rising or setting sun; the magnificent spectacle of the boundless ocean, sometimes so grand in its peaceful tranquillity, at others so majestic in its mighty power; the forests agitated by the storm, or alive with the song of birds; nor the glaciers and mountains—there are doubtless some whom none of these magnificent spectacles can move, whom "all the glories of heaven and earth may pass in daily succession without touching their hearts or elevating their minds." [1]

Such men are indeed pitiable. But, happily, they are exceptions. If we can none of us as yet fully appreciate the beauties of Nature, we are beginning to do so more and more.

For most of us the early summer has a special charm. The very life is luxury. The air is full of scent, and sound, and sunshine, of the song of birds and the murmur of insects; the meadows gleam with golden buttercups, it almost seems as if one could see the grass grow and the buds open; the bees hum for very joy, and the air is full of a thousand scents, above all perhaps that of new-mown hay.

The exquisite beauty and delight of a fine summer day in the country has never perhaps been more truly, and therefore more beautifully, described than by Jefferies in his "Pageant of Summer." "I linger," he says, "in the midst of the long grass, the luxury of the leaves, and the song in the very air. I seem as if I could feel all the glowing life the sunshine gives and the south wind

[1] Beattie.

calls to being. The endless grass, the endless leaves, the immense strength of the oak expanding, the unalloyed joy of finch and blackbird; from all of them I receive a little. . . . In the blackbird's melody one note is mine; in the dance of the leaf shadows the formed maze is for me, though the motion is theirs; the flowers with a thousand faces have collected the kisses of the morning. Feeling with them, I receive some, at least, of their fulness of life. Never could I have enough; never stay long enough. . . . The hours when the mind is absorbed by beauty are the only hours when we really live, so that the longer we can stay among these things so much the more is snatched from inevitable Time. . . . These are the only hours that are not wasted—these hours that absorb the soul and fill it with beauty. This is real life, and all else is illusion, or mere endurance. To be beautiful and to be calm, without mental fear, is the ideal of Nature. If I cannot achieve it, at least I can think it."

This chapter is already so long that I cannot touch on the contrast and variety of the seasons, each with its own special charm and interest, as

"The daughters of the year
Dance into light and die into the shade."[1]

Our countrymen derive great pleasure from the animal kingdom, in hunting, shooting, and fishing, thus obtaining fresh air and exercise, and being

[1] Tennyson.

led into much varied and beautiful scenery. Still it will probably ere long be recognized that even from a purely selfish point of view, killing animals is not the way to get the greatest enjoyment from them. How much more interesting would every walk in the country be, if Man would but treat other animals with kindness, so that they might approach us without fear, and we might have the constant pleasure of watching their winning ways. Their origin and history, structure and habits, senses and intelligence, offer an endless field of interest and wonder.

The richness of life is wonderful. Any one who will sit down quietly on the grass and watch a little will be indeed surprised at the number and variety of living beings, every one with a special history of its own, every one offering endless problems of great interest.

"If indeed thy heart were right, then would every creature be to thee a mirror of life, and a book of holy doctrine." [1]

The study of Natural History has the special advantage of carrying us into the country and the open air.

Not but what towns are beautiful too. They teem with human interest and historical associations.

Wordsworth was an intense lover of nature; yet does he not tell us, in lines which every Londoner will appreciate, that he knew nothing in nature

[1] Thomas à Kempis.

more fair, no calm more deep, than the city of London at early dawn?

> "Earth has not anything to show more fair;
> Dull would he be of soul who could pass by
> A sight so touching in its majesty:
> This City now doth, like a garment, wear
> The beauty of the morning; silent, bare,
> Ships, towers, domes, theatres, and temples lie
> Open unto the fields, and to the sky;
> All bright and glittering in the smokeless air.
> Never did sun more beautifully steep
> In his first splendor, valley, rock, or hill;
> Ne'er saw I, never felt, a calm so deep!
> The river glideth at its own sweet will:
> Dear God! the very houses seem asleep;
> And all that mighty heart is lying still!"

Milton also described London as

> "Too blest abode, no loveliness we see
> In all the earth, but it abounds in thee."

But after being some time in a great city, one feels a longing for the country.

> "The meanest floweret of the vale,
> The simplest note that swells the gale,
> The common sun, the air, the skies,
> To him are opening paradise." [1]

Here Gray justly places flowers in the first place, for when in any great town we think of the country, flowers seem first to suggest themselves.

[1] Gray.

"Flowers," says Ruskin, "seem intended for the solace of ordinary humanity. Children love them; quiet, tender, contented, ordinary people love them as they grow; luxurious and disorderly people rejoice in them gathered. They are the cottager's treasure; and in the crowded town, mark, as with a little broken fragment of rainbow, the windows of the workers in whose heart rests the covenant of peace." But in the crowded street, or even in the formal garden, flowers always seem, to me at least, as if they were pining for the freedom of the woods and fields, where they can live and grow as they please.

There are flowers for almost all seasons and all places. Flowers for spring, summer, and autumn, while even in the very depth of winter here and there one makes its appearance. There are flowers of the fields and woods and hedgerows, of the seashore and the lake's margin, of the mountain-side up to the very edge of the eternal snow.

And what an infinite variety they present.

> "Daffodils,
> That come before the swallow dares, and take
> The winds of March with beauty; violets, dim,
> But sweeter than the lids of Juno's eyes,
> Or Cytherea's breath; pale primroses,
> That die unmarried, ere they can behold
> Bright Phœbus in his strength, a malady
> Most incident to maids; bold oxlips and
> The crown imperial; lilies of all kinds,
> The flower-de-luce being one." [1]

[1] Shakespeare.

Nor are they mere delights to the eye; they are full of mystery and suggestions. They almost seem like enchanted princesses waiting for some princely deliverer. Wordsworth tells us that

> "To me the meanest flower that blows can give
> Thoughts that do often lie too deep for tears."

Every color again, every variety of form, has some purpose and explanation.

And yet, lovely as Flowers are, Leaves add even more to the Beauty of Nature. Trees in our northern latitudes seldom own large flowers; and though of course there are notable exceptions, such as the Horse-chestnut, still even in these cases the flowers live only a few days, while the leaves last for months. Every tree indeed is a picture in itself: The gnarled and rugged Oak, the symbol and source of our navy, sacred to the memory of the Druids, the type of strength, the sovereign of British trees; the Chestnut, with its beautiful, tapering, and rich green, glossy leaves, its delicious fruit, and to the durability of which we owe the grand and historic roof of Westminster Abbey.

The Birch is the queen of trees, with her feathery foliage, scarcely visible in spring but turning to leaves of gold in autumn; the pendulous twigs tinged with purple, and silver stems so brilliantly marked with black and white.

The Elm forms grand masses of foliage which turn a beautiful golden yellow in autumn; and the

Black Poplar with its perpendicular leaves, rustling and trembling with every breath of wind, towers over most other forest trees.

The Beech enlivens the country by its tender green in spring, rich green in summer, and glorious gold and orange in autumn, set off by the graceful gray stems; and has moreover, such a wealth of leaves that in autumn there are enough not only to clothe the tree itself but to cover the grass underneath.

If the Beech owes much to its delicate gray stem, even more beautiful is the reddish crimson of the Scotch Pines, in such charming contrast with the rich green of the foliage, by which it is shown off rather than hidden; and, with the green spires of the Firs, they keep the woods warm in winter.

Nor must I overlook the smaller trees: the Yew with its thick green foliage; the wild Guelder rose, which lights up the woods in autumn with translucent glossy berries and many-tinted leaves: or the Bryonies, the Briar, the Traveler's Joy, and many another plant, even humbler perhaps, and yet each with some exquisite beauty and grace of its own, so that we must all have sometimes felt our hearts overflowing with gladness and gratitude, as if the woods were full of music—as if

"The woods were filled so full with song
There seemed no room for sense of wrong."[1]

[1] Tennyson.

On the whole no doubt, woodlands are less beautiful in the winter: yet even then the delicate tracery of the branches, which cannot be so well seen when they are clothed with leaves, has a special beauty of its own; while every now and then hoar frost or snow settles like silver on every branch and twig, lighting up the forest as if by enchantment in preparation for some fairy festival.

I feel with Jefferies that "by day or by night, summer or winter, beneath trees the heart feels nearer to that depth of life which the far sky means. The rest of spirit found only in beauty, ideal and pure, comes there because the distance seems within touch of thought."

The general effect of forests in tropical regions must be very different from that of those in our latitudes. Kingsley describes it as one of helplessness, confusion, awe, all but terror. The trunks are very lofty and straight, and rising to a great height without a branch, so that the wood seems at first comparatively open. In Brazilian forests, for instance, the trees struggle upward, and the foliage forms an unbroken canopy, perhaps a hundred feet overhead. Here, indeed, high up in the air is the real life of the forest. Everything seems to climb to the light. The quadrupeds climb, birds climb, reptiles climb, and the variety of climbing plants is far greater than anything to which we are accustomed.

Many savage nations worship trees, and I really

think my first feeling would be one of delight and interest rather than of surprise, if some day when I am alone in a wood one of the trees were to speak to me. Even by day there is something mysterious in a forest, and this is much more the case at night.

With wood, water seems to be naturally associated. Without water no landscape is complete, while overhead the clouds add beauty to the heavens themselves. The spring and the rivulet, the brook, the river, and the lake, seem to give life to Nature, and were indeed regarded by our ancestors as living entities themselves. Water is beautiful in the morning mist, in the broad lake, in the glancing stream or the river pool, in the wide ocean, beautiful in all its varied moods. Water nourishes vegetation; it clothes the lowlands with green and the mountains with snow. It sculptures the rocks and excavates the valleys, in most cases acting mainly through the soft rain, though our harder rocks are still grooved by the ice-chisel of bygone ages.

The refreshing pour of water upon the earth is scarcely greater than that which it exercises on the mind of man. After a long spell of work how delightful it is to sit by a lake or river, or on the sea-ore, and enjoy

"A little murmur in mine ear,
A little ripple at my feet."[1]

[1] Trench.

Every Englishman loves the sight of the Sea. We feel that it is to us a second home. It seems to vivify the very atmosphere, so that Sea air is proverbial as a tonic, and makes the blood dance in our veins. The Ocean gives an impression of freedom and grandeur more intense perhaps than the aspect of the heavens themselves. A poor woman from Manchester, on being taken to the seaside, is said to have expressed her delight on seeing for the first time something of which there was enough for everybody. The sea coast is always interesting. When we think of the cliff sections with their histories of bygone ages; the shore itself teeming with seaweeds and animals, waiting for the return of the tide, or thrown up from deeper water by the waves; the weird cries of seabirds; the delightful feeling that with every breath we are laying in a store of fresh life, and health, and energy, it is impossible to over-estimate all we owe to the sea.

It is, moreover, always changing. We went for our holiday this year to Lyme Regis. Let me attempt to describe the changes in the view from our windows during a single day. Our sitting-room opened on to a little lawn, beyond which the ground drops suddenly to the sea, while over about two miles of water were the hills of the Dorsetshire coast—Golden Cap, with its bright crest of yellow sand, and the dark blue Lias Cliff of Black Ven. When I came early down in the morning the sun was rising opposite, shining into the room over a calm sea, along an avenue of light; by degrees, as it rose, the whole sea was gilt with light, and the hills bathed in a violet mist. By breakfast-time all color had faded from the sea—it was like silver passing on each side into gray; the sky was blue, flecked with fleecy clouds; while, on the gentler slopes of the coast opposite, fields and woods, and quarries and lines of stratification begin to show themselves, though the cliffs are still in shadow, and the more distant headlands still a mere succession of ghosts, each one fainter than the one before it. As the morning advances the sea becomes blue, the dark woods, green meadows, and golden cornfields of the opposite coast more distinct, and the details of the cliffs come gradually into view, and fishing-boats with dark sails begin to appear.

Gradually the sun rises higher, a yellow line of shore appears under the opposite cliffs, and the sea changes its color, mapping itself out as it were, the shallower parts turquoise blue, almost green; the deeper ones deep violet.

This does not last long—a thunderstorm comes up. The wind mutters overhead, the rain patters on the leaves, the coast opposite seems to shrink into itself, as if it would fly from the storm. The sea grows dark and rough, and white horses appear here and there.

But the storm is soon over. The clouds break, the rain stops, the sun shines once more, the hills opposite come out again. They are divided now not only into fields and woods, but into sunshine and shadow. The sky clears, and as the sun begins to descend westwards the sea becomes one beautiful clear uniform azure, changing again soon to pale blue in front and dark violet beyond ; and once more as clouds begin to gather again, into an archipelago of bright blue sea and deep islands of ultramarine. As the sun travels westward, the opposite hills change again. They scarcely seem like the same country. What was in sun is now in shade, and what was in shade now lies bright in the sunshine. The sea once more becomes a uniform solid blue, only flecked in places by scuds of wind, and becoming paler towards evening as the sun sinks, the cliffs which catch his setting rays losing their deep color and in some places looking almost as white as chalk, while at sunset they light up again for a moment with a golden glow, the sea at the same time sinking to a cold gray. But soon the hills grow cold too, Golden Cap holding out bravely to the last, and the shades of evening settle over cliff and wood, cornfield and meadow.

These are but a part, and a very small part, of the changes of a single day. And scarce any two days are alike. At times a sea-fog covers everything. Again the sea which sleeps to-day so peacefully sometimes rages, and the very existence of the bay itself bears witness to its force.

The night, again, varies like the day. Sometimes shrouded by a canopy of darkness, sometimes lit up by millions of brilliant worlds, sometimes bathed in the light of a moon, which never retains the same form for two nights together.

If Lakes are less grand than the sea, they are in some respects even more lovely. The seashore is comparatively bare. The banks of Lakes are often richly clothed with vegetation which comes close down to the water's edge, sometimes hanging even into the water itself. They are often studded with well-wooded islands. They are sometimes fringed with green meadows, sometimes bounded by rocky promontories rising directly from comparatively deep water, while the calm bright surface is often fretted by a delicate pattern of interlacing ripples, or reflects a second, softened, and inverted landscape.

To water again we owe the marvellous spectacle of the rainbow—"God's bow in the clouds." It is indeed truly a heavenly messenger, and so unlike anything else that it scarcely seems to belong to this world.

Many things are colored, but the rainbow seems to be color itself.

> "First the flaming red
> Sprang vivid forth; the tawny orange next,
> And next delicious yellow; by whose side
> Fell the kind beams of all-refreshing green.
> Then the pure blue that swells autumnal skies,
> Ethereal play'd; and then, of sadder hue
> Emerged the deeper indigo (as when
> The heavy-skirted evening droops with frost),
> While the last gleamings of refracted light
> Died in the fainting violet away."[1]

[1] Thomson.

We do not, I think, sufficiently realize how wonderful is the blessing of color. It would have been possible, it would even seem more probable, that though light might have enabled us to perceive objects, this could only have been by shade and form. How we perceive color it is very difficult to comprehend, and yet when we speak of beauty, among the ideas which come to us most naturally are those of birds and butterflies, flowers and shells, precious stones, skies, and rainbows.

Our minds might have been constituted exactly as they are, we might have been capable of comprehending the highest and sublimest truths, and yet, but for a small organ in the head, the world of sound would have been shut out from us; we should have lost the sounds of nature, the charms of music, the conversation of friends, and have been condemned to perpetual silence: and yet a slight alteration in the retina, which is not thicker than a sheet of paper, not larger than a finger nail,—and the glorious spectacle of this beautiful world, the exquisite variety of form, the glory and play of color, the variety of scenery, of woods and fields, and lakes and hills, seas and mountains, the glory of the sky alike by day and night, would all have been lost to us.

Mountains, again, "seem to have been built for the human race, as at once their schools and cathedrals; full of treasures of illuminated manuscript for the scholar, kindly in simple lessons for the worker, quiet in pale cloisters for the thinker,

THE BEAUTY OF NATURE. 255

glorious in holiness for the worshipper. And of these great cathedrals of the earth, with their gates of rock, pavements of cloud, choirs of stream and stone, altars of snow, and vaults of purple traversed by the continual stars."[1]

All these beauties are comprised in Tennyson's exquisite description of Œnone's vale—the city, flowers, trees, river, and mountains.

> "There is a vale in Ida, lovelier
> Than all the valleys of Ionian hills.
> The swimming vapor slopes athwart the glen,
> Puts forth an arm, and creeps from pine to pine,
> And loiters, slowly drawn. On either hand
> The lawns and meadow-ledges midway down
> Hang rich in flowers, and far below them roars
> The long brook falling thro' the clov'n ravine
> In cataract after cataract to the sea.
> Behind the valley topmost Gargarus
> Stands up and takes the morning; but in front
> The gorges, opening wide apart, reveal
> Troas and Ilion's column'd citadel,
> The crown of Troas."

And when we raise our eyes from earth, who has not sometimes felt " the witchery of the soft blue sky; " who has not watched a cloud floating upward as if on its way to heaven, or when

> "Sunbeam proof, I hang like a roof
> The mountain its columns be."[2]

[1] Ruskin.   [2] Shelley.

And yet " if, in our moments of utter idleness and insipidity, we turn to the sky as a last resource, which of its phenomena do we speak of? One says, it has been wet; and another, it has been windy; and another, it has been warm. Who, among the whole chattering crowd, can tell me of the forms and the precipices of the chain of tall white mountains that girded the horizon at noon yesterday? Who saw the narrow sunbeam that came out of the south, and smote upon their summits until they melted and mouldered away in a dust of blue rain? Who saw the dance of the dead clouds when the sunlight left them last night, and the west wind blew them before it like withered leaves? All has passed, unregretted as unseen; or if the apathy be ever shaken off, even for an instant, it is only by what is gross, or what is extraordinary; and yet it is not in the broad and fierce manifestations of the elemental energies, not in the clash of the hail, nor the drift of the whirlwind, that the highest characters of the sublime are developed."[1]

But exquisitely lovely as is the blue arch of the midday sky, with its inexhaustible variety of clouds, " there is yet a light which the eye invariably seeks with a deeper feeling of the beautiful, the light of the declining or breaking day, and the flakes of scarlet cloud burning like watch-fires in the green sky of the horizon."[2]

[1] Ruskin. [2] *Ibid.*

The evening colors indeed soon fade away, but as night comes on,

> "How glorious the firmament
> With living sapphires! Hesperus that led
> The starry host, rode brightest; till the moon
> Rising in clouded majesty, at length,
> Apparent queen, unveiled her peerless light,
> And o'er the dark her silver mantle threw."[1]

We generally speak of a beautiful night when it is calm and clear, and the stars shine brightly overhead; but how grand also are the wild ways of Nature, how magnificent when the lightning flashes, "between gloom and glory;" when

> "From peak to peak, the rattling crags among
> Leaps the live thunder."[2]

In the words of Ossian—

> "Ghosts ride in the tempest to-night;
> Sweet is their voice between the gusts of wind,
> Their songs are of other worlds."

Nor are the wonders and beauties of the heavens limited by the clouds and the blue sky, lovely as they are. In the heavenly bodies we have before us "the perpetual presence of the sublime." They are so immense and so far away, and yet on soft summer nights "they seem leaning down to whisper in the ear of our souls."[3]

[1] Wordsworth.   [2] Swinburne.   [3] Symonds.

"A man can hardly lift up his eyes toward the heavens," says Seneca, "without wonder and veneration, to see so many millions of radiant lights, and to observe their courses and revolutions, even without any respect to the common good of the Universe."

Who does not sympathize with the feelings of Dante as he rose from his visit to the lower regions, until, he says,

> "On our view the beautiful lights of heaven
> Dawned through a circular opening in the cave,
> Thence issuing, we again beheld the stars."

As we watch the stars at night they seem so still and motionless that we can hardly realize that all the time they are rushing on with a velocity far far exceeding any that man has ever accomplished.

Like the sands of the sea, the stars of heaven have ever been used as an appropriate symbol of number, and we know that there are some 75,000,000, many, no doubt, with planets of their own. But this is by no means all. The floor of heaven is not only "thick inlaid with patines of bright gold," but is studded also with extinct stars, once probably as brilliant as our own sun, but now dead and cold, as Helmholtz tells us our sun itself will be some seventeen millions of years hence. Then, again, there are the comets, which, though but few are visible to us at once, are even more numerous than the stars; there are the nebulæ, and the countless minor bodies circulating in space, and occasionally visible as meteors.

Nor is it only the number of the heavenly bodies which is so overwhelming; their magnitude and distances are almost more impressive. The ocean is so deep and broad as to be almost infinite, and indeed in so far as our imagination is the limit, so it may be. Yet what is the ocean compared to the sky? Our globe is little compared to the giant orbs of Jupiter and Saturn, which again sink into insignificance by the side of the sun. The sun itself is almost as nothing compared with the dimensions of the solar system. Sirius is calculated to be a thousand times as great as the Sun, and a million times as far away. The solar system itself travels in one region of space, sailing between worlds and worlds, and is surrounded by many other systems as great and complex as itself; and we know that even then we have not reached the limits of the Universe itself.

There are stars so distant that their light, though traveling 180,000 miles in a second, yet takes years to reach us; and beyond all these are other systems of stars which are so far away that they cannot be perceived singly, but even in our most powerful telescopes appear only as minute clouds or nebulæ. It is, indeed, but a feeble expression of the truth to say that the infinities revealed to us by Science,—the infinitely great in the one direction, and the infinitely small in the other,—go far beyond anything which had occurred to the unaided imagination of Man, and are not only a never-failing source of pleasure and interest, but seem to lift us out of the petty troubles and sorrows of life.

CHAPTER IX.

THE TROUBLES OF LIFE.

CHAPTER IX.

THE TROUBLES OF LIFE.

WE have in life many troubles, and troubles are of many kinds. Some sorrows, alas, are real enough, especially those we bring on ourselves, but others, and by no means the least numerous, are mere ghosts of troubles: if we face them boldly, we find that they have no substance or reality, but are mere creations of our own morbid imagination, and that it is as true now as in the time of David that " Man disquieteth himself in a vain shadow."

Some, indeed, of our troubles are evils, but not real; while others are real, but not evils.

"And yet, into how unfathomable a gulf the mind rushes when the troubles of this world agitate it. If it then forget its own light, which is eternal joy, and rush into the outer darkness, which are the cares of this world, as the mind now does, it knows nothing else but lamentations." [1]

"Athens," said Epictetus, "is a good place,— but happiness is much better; to be free from passions, free from disturbance."

[1] King Alfred's translations of the *Consolations of Bœthius*.

We should endeavor to maintain ourselves in

> "That blessed mood
> In which the burden of the mystery,
> In which the heavy and the weary weight,
> Of all this unintelligible world
> Is lightened."[1]

So shall we fear "neither the exile of Aristides, nor the prison of Anaxagoras, nor the poverty of Socrates, nor the condemnation of Phocion, but think virtue worthy our love even under such trials."[2] We should then be, to a great extent, independent of external circumstances, for

> "Stone walls do not a prison make,
> Nor iron bars a cage,
> Minds innocent and quiet take
> That for a hermitage.
>
> "If I have freedom in my love,
> And in my soul am free;
> Angels alone that soar above
> Enjoy such liberty."[3]

Happiness indeed depends much more on what is within than without us. When Hamlet says the world is "a goodly prison; in which there are many confines, wards, and dungeons; Denmark being one of the worst," and Rosencrantz differs from him, he rejoins wisely, "Why then, 'tis none to you: for there is nothing either good or bad,

---

[1] Wordsworth. [2] Plutarch. [3] Lovelace.

but thinking makes it so: to me it is a prison."
"All is opinion," said Marcus Aurelius. "That which does not make a man worse, how can it make his life worse? But death certainly, and life, honor and dishonor, pain and pleasure, all these things happen equally to good men and bad, being things which make us neither better nor worse."

"The greatest evils," says Jeremy Taylor, "are from within us; and from ourselves also we must look for our greatest good."

"The mind," says Milton,

"is its own place, and in itself
Can make a Heaven of Hell, a Hell of Heaven."

Milton indeed in his blindness saw more beautiful visions, and Beethoven in his deafness heard more heavenly music, than most of us can ever hope to enjoy.

We are all apt, when we know not what may happen, to fear the worst. When we know the full extent of any danger, it is half over. Hence, we dread ghosts more than robbers, not only without reason, but against reason; for even if ghosts existed, how could they hurt us? and in ghost stories, few, even those who say that they have seen a ghost, ever profess or pretend to have felt one.

Milton, in his description of death, dwells on this characteristic of obscurity:

"The other shape,
If shape it might be call'd that shape had none
Distinguishable, in member, joint, or limb;
Or substance might be call'd that shadow seem'd,
For each seem'd either; black he stood as night;
Fierce as ten furies; terrible as hell;
And shook a deadly dart. What seem'd his head
The likeness of a kingly crown had on."

The effect of darkness and night in enhancing terrors is dwelt on in one of the sublimest passages in Job—

" In thoughts from the visions of the night,
When deep sleep falleth on men,
Fear came upon me, and trembling,
Which made all my bones to shake.
Then a spirit passed before my face;
The hair of my flesh stood up.
It stood still, an image was before mine eyes.
There was silence; and I heard a voice saying
Shall mortal man be more just than God?"

Thus was the terror turned into a lesson of comfort and of mercy.

We often magnify troubles and difficulties, and look at them till they seem much greater than they really are.

" Dangers are no more light, if they once seem light; and more dangers have deceived men than forced them: nay, it were better to meet some dangers half way, though they come nothing near, than to keep too long a watch upon their approaches; for if a man watch too long, it is odds he will fall asleep."[1]

Foresight is very wise, but foresorrow is very foolish; and castles are at any rate better than dungeons, in the air.

Some of our troubles, no doubt, are real enough, but yet are not evils.

It happens, unfortunately too often, that by some false step, intentional or unintentional, we have missed the right road, and gone wrong. Can we then retrace our steps? can we recover what is lost? This may be done. It is too gloomy a view to affirm that

> A word too much, or a kiss too long,
> And the world is never the same again."

There are two noble sayings of Socrates, that to do evil is more to be avoided than to suffer it; and that when a man has done evil, it is better for him to be punished than to be unpunished.

We generally speak of selfishness as a fault, and as if it interfered with the general happiness. But this is not altogether correct.

The pity is that so many people are foolishly selfish: that they pursue a course of action which neither makes themselves nor any one else happy.

"Every man," says Goethe, "ought to begin with himself, and make his own happiness first, from which the happiness of the whole world would

[1] Bacon.

at last unquestionably follow." It is easy to say that this is too broadly stated, and of course exceptions might be pointed out: but if every one would avoid excess, and take care of his own health; would keep himself strong and cheerful; would make his home happy, and give no cause for the petty vexations which embitter domestic life; would attend to his own affairs and keep himself sober and solvent; would, in the words of the Chinese proverb, "sweep away the snow from before his own door, and never mind the frost upon his neighbor's tiles;" though it might not be the noblest course of conduct; still, how well it would be for their family, relations, and friends. But, unfortunately,

> " Look round the habitable world, how few
> Know their own good, or, knowing it, pursue." [1]

It would be a great thing if people could be brought to realize that they can never add to the sum of their happiness by doing wrong. In the case of children, indeed, we recognize this; we perceive that a spoilt child is not a happy one; that it would have been far better for him to have been punished at first and thus saved from greater suffering in after life.

It is a beautiful idea that every man has with him a Guardian Angel; and it is true too: for

[1] Dryden.

THE TROUBLES OF LIFE.

Conscience is ever on the watch, ever ready to warn us of danger.

We often feel disposed to complain, and yet it is most ungrateful:

> For who would lose,
> Though full of pain, this intellectual being,
> Those thoughts that wander through Eternity;
> To perish rather, swallowed up, and lost
> In the wide womb of uncreated thought."[1]

But perhaps it will be said that we are sent here in preparation for another and a better world. Well, then, why should we complain of what is but a preparation for future happiness?

We ought to

> "Count each affliction, whether light or grave,
>   God's messenger sent down to thee; do thou
>   With courtesy receive him; rise and bow;
> And, ere his shadow pass thy threshold, crave
> Permission first his heavenly feet to lave;
>   Then lay before him all thou hast; allow
>   No cloud of passion to usurp thy brow,
> Or mar thy hospitality; no wave
> Of mortal tumult to obliterate
>   The soul's marmoreal calmness: Grief shall be
> Like joy, majestic, equable, sedate;
>   Confirming, cleansing, raising, making free;
> Strong to consume small troubles; to commend
> Great thoughts, grave thoughts, thoughts lasting to the end."[2]

[1] Milton. [2] Aubrey de Vere.

Some persons are like the waters of Siloam, and require to be troubled before they can exercise their virtue.

"We shall get more contentedness," says Plutarch, "from the presence of all these blessings if we fancy them as absent, and remember from time to time how people when ill yearn for health, and people in war for peace, and strangers and unknown in a great city for reputation and friends, and how painful it is to be deprived of all these when one has once had them. For then each of these blessings will not appear to us only great and valuable when it is lost, and of no value when we have it. . . . And yet it makes much for contentedness of mind to look for the most part at home and to our own condition; or if not, to look at the case of people worse off than ourselves, and not, as people do, to compare ourselves with those who are better off. . . . But you will find others, Chians, or Galatians, or Bithynians, not content with the share of glory or power they have among their fellow-citizens, but weeping because they do not wear senators' shoes; or, if they have them, that they cannot be prætors of Rome; or if they get that office, that they are not consuls; or if they are consuls, that they are only proclaimed second and not first. . . . Whenever, then, you admire any one carried by in his litter as a greater man than yourself, lower your eyes and look at those that bear the litter." And again, "I am very taken with Diogenes' remark to a stranger at

Lacedæmon, who was dressing with much display for a feast, 'Does not a good man consider every day a feast?' . . . Seeing then that life is the most complete initiation into all these things, it ought to be full of ease of mind and joy;" and if properly understood, would enable us "to acquiesce in the present without repining, to remember the past with thankfulness, and to meet the future hopefully and cheerfully without fear of suspicion."

CHAPTER X.

LABOR AND REST.

"Through labor to rest, through combat to victory."
                                    THOMAS À KEMPIS.

CHAPTER X.

LABOR AND REST.

AMONG the troubles of life I do not, of course, reckon the necessity of labor.

Work indeed, and hard work, if only it is in moderation, is in itself a rich source of happiness. We all know how quickly time passes when we are well employed, while the moments hang heavily on the hands of the idle. Occupation drives away care and all the small troubles of life. The busy man has no time to brood or to fret.

> " From toil he wins his spirits light,
> From busy day the peaceful night;
> Rich, from the very want of wealth,
> In Heaven's best treasures, peace and health." [1]

This applies especially to the labor of the field and the workshop. Humble it may be, but if it does not dazzle with the promise of fame, it gives the satisfaction of duty fulfilled, and the inestimable blessing of health. As Emerson reminds those entering life, " The angels that live with them, and are weaving laurels of life for their youthful brows, are toil and truth and mutual faith."

[1] Gray.

Labor was truly said by the ancients to be the price which the gods set upon everything worth having. We all admit, though we often forget, the marvellous power of perseverance, and yet all Nature, down to Bruce's spider, is continually impressing this lesson on us.

Hard writing, it has been said, makes easy reading; Plato is said to have rewritten the first page of the *Republic* thirteen times; and Carlo Maratti, we are told, sketched the head of Antinoüs three hundred times before he wrought it to his satisfaction.

It is better to wear out than to rust out, and there is "a dust which settles on the heart, as well as that which rests upon the ledge." [1]

But though labor is good for man, it may be, and unfortunately often is, carried to excess. Many are wearily asking themselves

"Ah why
Should life all labor be?" [2]

There is a time for all things, says Solomon, a time to work and a time to play: we shall work all the better for reasonable change, and one reward of work is to secure leisure.

It is a good saying that where there's a will there's a way; but while it is all very well to wish, wishes must not take the place of work.

[1] Jefferies.　　　　[2] Tennyson.

In whatever sphere his duty lies every man must rely mainly on himself. Others can help us, but we must make ourselves. No one else can see for us. To profit by our advantages we must learn to use for ourselves

"The dark lantern of the spirit
Which none can see by, but he who bears it."

It is hardly an exaggeration to say that honest work is never thrown away. If we do not find the imaginary treasure, at any rate we enrich the vineyard.

"Work," says Nature to man, "in every hour, paid or unpaid; see only that thou work, and thou canst not escape the reward: whether thy work be fine or coarse, planting corn or writing epics, so only it be honest work, done to thine own approbation, it shall earn a reward to the senses as well as to the thought: no matter how often defeated, you are born to victory. The reward of a thing well done is to have done it." [1]

Nor can any work, however persevering, or any success, however great, exhaust the prizes of life.

The most studious, the most successful, must recognize that there yet remain

"So much to do that is not e'en begun,
So much to hope for that we cannot see,
So much to win, so many things to be." [2]

[1] Emerson. [2] Morris.

At the present time, though there may be some special drawbacks, still we come to our work with many advantages which were not enjoyed in olden times. We live in much greater security ourselves, and are less liable to have the fruits of our labor torn violently from us.

In olden times the difficulties of study were far greater than they are now. Books were expensive and cumbersome, in many cases moreover chained to the desks on which they were kept. The greatest scholars have often been very poor. Erasmus used to read by moonlight because he could not afford a candle, and " begged a penny, not for the love of charity, but for the love of learning." [1]

Want of time is no excuse for idleness. "Our life," says Jeremy Taylor, " is too short to serve the ambition of a haughty prince or a usurping rebel; too little time to purchase great wealth, to satisfy the pride of a vainglorious fool, to trample upon all the enemies of our just or unjust interest: but for the obtaining virtue, for the purchase of sobriety and modesty, for the actions of religion, God gives us time sufficient, if we make the outgoings of the morning and evening, that is our infancy and old age, to be taken into the computations of a man."

Work is so much a necessity of existence, that it is less a question whether, than how, we shall work. An old proverb tells us that the Devil finds work for those who do not make it for themselves.

[1] Coleridge.

If we Englishmen have succeeded as a race, it has been due in no small measure to the fact that we have worked hard. Not only so, but we have induced the forces of Nature to work for us. "Steam," says Emerson, "is almost an Englishman."

The power of work has especially characterized our greatest men. Cecil said of Sir W. Raleigh that he "could toil terribly."

We are most of us proud of belonging to the greatest Empire the world has ever seen. It may be said of us with especial truth in Wordsworth's words that

> "The world is too much with us; late and soon
> Getting and spending, we lay waste our powers."

Yes, but what world? The world will be with us sure enough, and whether we please or not. But what sort of world it will be for us will depend greatly on ourselves.

We are told to pray not to be taken out of the world, but to be kept from the evil.

There are various ways of working. Quickness may be good, but haste is bad.

> "Wie das Gestirn
> Ohne Hast
> Ohne Rast
> Drehe sich Jeder
> Um die eigne Last."[1]

[1] Goethe.

"Like a star, without haste, without rest, let every one fulfil his own hest."

Newton is reported to have described as his mode of working that "I keep the subject constantly before me, and wait till the first dawnings open slowly by little and little into a full and clear light."

"The secret of genius," says Emerson, "is to suffer no fiction to exist for us; to realize all that we know; in the high refinement of modern life, in Arts, in Sciences, in books, in men, to exact good faith, reality, and a purpose; and first, last, midst, and without end, to honor every truth by use."

Lastly, work secures the rich reward of rest, we must rest to be able to work well, and work to be able to enjoy rest.

"We must no doubt beware that our rest become not the rest of stones, which so long as they are torrent-tossed and thunder-stricken maintain their majesty; but when the stream is silent, and the storm past, suffer the grass to cover them, and the lichen to feed on them, and are ploughed down into the dust. . . . The rest which is glorious is of the chamois couched breathless in its granite bed, not of the stalled ox over his fodder."[1]

When we have done our best we may wait the result without anxiety.

"What hinders a man, who has clearly comprehended these things, from living with a light heart

[1] Ruskin.

and bearing easily the reins; quietly expecting everything which can happen, and enduring that which has already happened? Would you have me to bear poverty? Come and you will know what poverty is when it has found one who can act well the part of a poor man. Would you have me to possess power? Let me have the power, and also the trouble of it. Well, banishment? Wherever I shall go, there it will be well with me." [1]

The Buddhists believe in many forms of future punishment; but the highest reward of virtue is Nirvana—the final and eternal rest.

Very touching is the appeal of Ashmanezer to be left in peace, which was engraved on his Sarcophagus at Sidon,—now in Paris.

"In the month of Bul, the fourteenth year of my reign, I, King Ashmanezer, King of the Sidonians, son of King Tabuith, King of the Sidonians, spake, saying: 'I have been stolen away before my time—a son of the flood of days. The whilom great is dumb; the son of gods is dead. And I rest in this grave, even in this tomb, in the place which I have built. My adjuration to all the Ruling Powers and all men: Let no one open this resting-place, nor search for treasure, for there is no treasure with us; and let him not bear away the couch of my rest, and not trouble us in this resting-place by disturbing the couch of my slumbers. . . . For all men who should open the tomb of my rest, or any man who should carry away the

[1] Epictetus.

couch of my rest, or any one who trouble me on this couch: unto them there shall be no rest with the departed: they shall not be buried in a grave, and there shall be to them neither son nor seed. . . . There shall be to them neither root below nor fruit above, nor honor among the living under the sun.'"[1]

The idle man does not know what it is to rest. Hard work, moreover, tends not only to give us rest for the body, but, what is even more important, peace to the mind. If we have done our best to do, and to be, we can rest in peace.

"En la sua voluntade é nostra pace."[2] In His will is our peace; and in such peace the mind will find its truest delight, for

"When care sleeps, the soul wakes."

In youth, as is right enough, the idea of exertion, and of struggles, is inspiring and delightful; but as years advance the hope and prospect of peace and of rest gain ground gradually, and

"When the last dawns are fallen on gray,
And all life's toils and ease complete,
They know who work, not they who play,
If rest is sweet."[3]

[1] From Sir M. S. Gray Duff's *A Winter in Syria*.
[2] Dante. [3] Symonds.

CHAPTER XI.
RELIGION.

"For what doth the Lord require of thee, but to do justly, to love mercy, and to walk humbly with thy God."
—MICAH.

" Pure religion and undefiled is this, to visit the fatherless and widows in their affliction, and to keep himself unspotted from the world."—JAMES I.

"The letter killeth, but the spirit giveth life."
2 CORINTHIANS.

CHAPTER XI.

RELIGION.

IT would be quite out of place here to enter into any discussion of theological problems or to advocate any particular doctrines. Nevertheless I could not omit what is to most so great a comfort and support in sorrow and suffering, and a source of the purest happiness.

We commonly, however, bring together under this term two things which are yet very different: the religion of the heart, and that of the head. The first deals with conduct, and the duties of Man; the second with the nature of the supernatural and the future of the soul, being in fact a branch of knowledge.

Religion should be a strength, guide, and comfort, not a source of intellectual anxiety or angry argument. To persecute for religion's sake implies belief in a jealous, cruel, and unjust Deity. If we have done our best to arrive at the truth, to torment oneself about the result is to doubt the goodness of God, and, in the words of Bacon, "to bring down the Holy Ghost, instead of the likeness of a dove, in the shape of a raven."

"The letter killeth, but the spirit giveth life," and the first duty of religion is to form the highest possible conception of God.

Many a man, however, and still more many a woman, render themselves miserable on entering life by theological doubts and difficulties. These have reference, in ninety-nine cases out of a hundred, not to what we should do, but to what we should think. As regards action, conscience is generally a ready guide; to follow it is the real difficulty. Theology, on the other hand, is a most abstruse science; but as long as we honestly wish to arrive at truth we need not fear that we shall be punished for unintentional error. "For what," says Micah, "doth the Lord require of thee, but to do justly, to love mercy, and to walk humbly with thy God." There is very little theology in the Sermon on the Mount, or indeed in any part of the Gospels; and the differences which keep us apart have their origin rather in the study than the Church. Religion was intended to bring peace on earth and goodwill toward men, and whatever tends to hatred and persecution, however correct in the letter, must be utterly wrong in the spirit.

How much misery would have been saved to Europe if Christians had been satisfied with the Sermon on the Mount!

Bokhara is said to have contained more than three hundred colleges, all occupied with theology, but ignorant of everything else, and it was probably one of the most bigoted and uncharitable cities in the world. "Knowledge puffeth up, but charity edifieth."

We must not forget that

> "He prayeth best who loveth best
> All things both great and small."

Theologians too often appear to agree that

> "The awful shadow of some unseen power
> Floats, though unseen, among us";[1]

and in the days of the Inquisition many must have sighed for the cheerful child-like religion of the Greeks, if they could but have had the Nymphs and Nereids, the Fays and Faeries, with Destiny and Fate, but without Jupiter and Mars.

Sects are the work of Sectarians. No truly great religious teacher, as Carlyle said, ever intended to found a new Sect.

Diversity of worship, says a Persian proverb, "has divided the human race into seventy-two nations." From among all their dogmas I have selected one—"Divine Love." And again, "He needs no other rosary whose thread of life is strung with the beads of love and thought."

There is more true Christianity in some pagan Philosophers than in certain Christian theologians. Take, for instance, Plato, Marcus Aurelius, Epictetus, and Plutarch.

[1] Shelley.

"Now I, Callicles," says Socrates, "am persuaded of the truth of these things, and I consider how I shall present my soul whole and undefiled before the judge in that day. Renouncing the honors at which the world aims, I desire only to know the truth, and to live as well as I can, and, when the time comes, to die. And, to the utmost of my power, I exhort all other men to do the same. And in return for your exhortation of me, I exhort you also to take part in the great combat, which is the combat of life, and greater than every other earthly conflict."

"As to piety toward the Gods," says Epictetus, "you must know that this is the chief thing, to have right opinions about them, to think that they exist, and that they administer the All well and justly; and you must fix yourself in this principle (duty), to obey them, and to yield to them in everything which happens, and voluntarily to follow it as being accomplished by the wisest intelligence."

"Do not act," says Marcus Aurelius, "as if thou wert going to live ten thousand years. Death hangs over thee. While thou livest, while it is in thy power, be good. . . .

"Since it is possible that thou mayest depart from life this very moment, regulate every act and thought accordingly. But to go away from among men, if there be gods, is not a thing to be afraid of, for the gods will not involve thee in evil; but if indeed they do not exist, or if they have no concern about human affairs, what is it to me to live in a universe devoid of gods, or devoid of Providence. But in truth they do exist, and they do care for human things, and they have put all the means in man's power to enable him not to fall into real evils. And as for the rest, if there was anything evil, they would have provided for this also, that it should be altogether in a man's power not to fall into it."

And Plutarch: "The Godhead is not blessed by reason of his silver and gold, nor yet Almighty through his thunder and lightnings, but on account of knowledge and intelligence."

It is no doubt very difficult to arrive at the exact teaching of Eastern Moralists, but the same spirit runs through Oriental Literature. For instance, in the *Toy Cart*, when the wicked Prince wishes Vita to murder the Heroine, and says that no one would see him, Vita declares "All nature would behold the crime—the Genii of the Grove, the Sun, the Moon, the Winds, the Vault of Heaven, the firm-set Earth, the mighty Yama who judges the dead, and the conscious Soul."

Take even the most extreme type of difference. Is the man, says Plutarch, "a criminal who holds there are no gods; and is not he that holds them to be such as the superstitious believe them, is he not possessed with notions infinitely more atrocious? I for my part would much rather have men say of me that there never was a Plutarch at all, nor is now, than to say that Plutarch is a man inconstant, fickle, easily moved to anger, revengeful for trifling provocations, vexed at small things."

There is no doubt a tone of doubting sadness in Roman moralists, as in Hadrain's dying lines to his soul—

> "Animula, vagula, blandula
> Hospes, comesque corporis
> Qua nunc abibis in loca:
> Pallidula, rigida, nudula,
> Nec, ut soles, dabis jocos."

The same spirit indeed is expressed in the epitaph on the tomb of the Duke of Buckingham in Westminster Abbey—

> "Dubius non improbus vixi
> Incertus morior, non perturbatus;
> Humanum est nescire et errare,
> Deo confido
> Omnipotenti benevolentissimo:
> Ens entium miserere mei."

Many thing have been mistaken for religion, selfishness especially, but also fear, hope, love of music, of art, of pomp; scruples often take the place of love, and the glory of heaven is sometimes made to depend upon precious stones and jewelry. Many, as has been well said, run after Christ, not for the miracles, but for the loaves.

In many cases religious differences are mainly verbal. There is an Eastern tale of four men, an

Arab, a Persian, a Turk, and a Greek, who agreed to club together for an evening meal, but when they had done so they quarrelled as to what it should be. The Turk proposed Azum, the Arab Aneb, the Persian Anghur, while the Greek insisted on Stapylion. While they were disputing

> "Before their eyes did pass,
> Laden with grapes, a gardener's ass.
> Sprang to his feet each man, and showed,
> With eager hand, that purple load.
> 'See Azum,' said the Turk; and 'see
> Anghur,' the Persian; 'what should be
> Better.' 'Nay Aneb, Aneb 'tis,'
> The Arab cried. The Greek said, 'This
> Is my Stapylion.' Then they bought
> Their grapes in peace.
>   Hence be ye taught."[1]

It is said that on one occasion, when Dean Stanley had been explaining his views to Lord Beaconsfield, the latter replied, "Ah! Mr. Dean, that is all very well, but you must remember,—No dogmas, no Deans." To lose such Deans as Stanley would indeed be a great misfortune; but does it follow? Religions, far from being really built on Dogmas, are too often weighed down and crushed by them. No one can doubt that Stanley has done much to strengthen the Church of England.

[1] Arnold. *Pearls of the Faith.*

We may not always agree with Spinoza, but is he not right when he says, "The first precept of the divine law, therefore, indeed its sum and substance, is to love God unconditionally as the supreme good—unconditionally, I say, and not from any love or fear of aught besides"? And again, that the very essence of religion is belief in "a Supreme Being who delights in justice and mercy, whom all who would be saved are bound to obey, and whose worship consists in the practice of justice and charity toward our neighbors"?

Doubt is of two natures, and we often confuse a wise suspension of judgment with the weakness of hesitation. To profess an opinion for which we have no sufficient reason is clearly illogical, but when it is necessary to act we must do so on the best evidence available, however slight that may be. Herein lies the importance of common sense, the instincts of a General, the sagacity of a Statesman. Pyrrho, the recognized representative of doubt, was often wise in suspending his judgment, however foolish in hesitating to act, and in apologizing when, after resisting all the arguments of philosophy, an angry dog drove him from his position.

Collect from the Bible all that Christ thought necessary for his disciples, and how little Dogma there is. "Pure religion and undefiled is this, to visit the fatherless and widows in their affliction, and to keep himself unspotted from the world." "By this shall all men know that ye are my disciples, if ye have love one to another." "Suffer little children to come unto me." And one lesson which little children have to teach us is that religion is an affair of the heart and not of the mind only.

Why should we expect Religion to solve questions with reference to the origin and destiny of the Universe? We do not expect the most elaborate treatise to tell us the origin of electricity or of heat. Natural History throws no light on the origin of life. Has Biology ever professed to explain existence?

"Simonides was asked at Syracuse by Hiero, who or what God was, when he requested a day's time to think of his answer. On subsequent days he always doubled the period required for deliberation; and when Hiero inquired the reason, he replied that the longer he considered the subject, the more obscure it appeared."

The Vedas say, "In the midst of the sun is the light, in the midst of light is truth, and in the midst of truth is the imperishable being." Deity has been defined as a circle whose centre is everywhere, and whose circumference is nowhere, but the "God is love" of St. John appeals more forcibly to the human soul.

The Church is not a place for study or speculation. Few but can sympathize with Eugénie de Guréin in her tender affection for the little Chapel at Cahuze where she tells us she left " tant de misères."

Doubt does not exclude Faith.

> "Perplexed in faith, but pure in deeds
> At last he beat his music out.
> There lies more faith in honest doubt,
> Believe me, than in half the creeds." [1]

And if we must admit that many points are still, and probably long will be involved in obscurity, we may be pardoned if we indulge ourselves in various speculations both as to our beginning and our end.

> "Our birth is but a sleep and a forgetting;
> The soul that rises with us, our life's star
> Hath had elsewhere its setting,
> And cometh from afar;
> Not in entire forgetfulness,
> And not in utter nakedness,
> But trailing clouds of glory do we come
> From God who is our home." [2]

Unfortunately many have attempted to compound for wickedness in life by purity of belief, a vain and fruitless effort. To do right is the sure ladder which leads up to Heaven, though the true faith will help us to find and to climb it.

> "It is my duty to have loved the highest,
> It surely was my profit had I known,
> It would have been my pleasure had I seen."

[1] Tennyson.   [2] Wordsworth.

But though religious truth can justify no bitterness, it is well worth any amount of thought and study.

I hope I shall not be supposed to depreciate any honest effort to arrive at truth, or to undervalue the devotion of those who have died for their religion. But surely it is a mistake to regard martyrdom as a merit, when from their own point of view it was in reality a privilege.

Let every man be persuaded in his own mind

"Truth is the highest thing that man may keep." [1]

To arrive at truth we should spare ourselves no pain, but certainly inflict none on others.

We may be sure that quarrels will never advance religion, and that to persecute is no way to convert. No doubt those who consider that all who do not agree with them will suffer eternal torments, seem logically justified in persecution even unto death. Such a course, if carried out consistently, might stamp out a particular sect, and any sufferings which could be inflicted here would on this hypothesis be as nothing in comparison with the pains of Hell. Only it must be admitted that such a view of religion is incompatible with any faith in the goodness of God, and seems quite irreconcilable with the teaching of Christ.

Moreover, the Inquisition has even from its own

[1] Chaucer.

point of view proved generally a failure. The blood of the martyrs is the seed of the Church.

"In obedience to the order of the Council of Constance (1415) the remains of Wickliffe were exhumed and burnt to ashes, and these cast into the Swift, a neighboring brook running hard by, and thus this brook hath conveyed his ashes into Avon; Avon into Severn; Severn into the narrow seas; they into the main ocean. And thus the ashes of Wickliffe are the emblem of his doctrine, which now is dispersed all the world over."[1]

The Talmud says that when a man once asked Shamai to teach him the Law in one lesson, Shamai drove him away in anger. He then went to Hillel with the same request. Hillel said, "Do unto others as you would have others do unto you. This is the whole Law; the rest, merely Commentaries upon it."

The Religion of the lower races is almost as a rule one of terror and of dread. Their deities are jealous and revengeful, cruel, merciless, and selfish, hateful and yet childish. They require to be propitiated by feasts and offerings, often even by human sacrifices. They are not only exacting, but so capricious that, with the best intentions, it is often impossible to be sure of pleasing them. From such evil beings Sorcerers and Witches derived their hellish powers. No one was safe. No one knew where danger lurked. Actions apparently the most trifling might be fraught with ser-

[1] Fuller.

ious risk: objects apparently the most innocent might be fatal.

In many cases there are supposed to be deities of Crime, of Misfortunes, of Disease. These wicked Spirits naturally encourage evil rather than good. An energetic friend of mine was sent to a district in India where smallpox was specially prevalent, and where one of the principal Temples was dedicated to the Goddess of that disease. He had the people vaccinated, in spite of some opposition, and the disease disappeared, much to the astonishment of the natives. But the priests of the Deity of Smallpox were not disconcerted; only they deposed the Image of their discomfited Goddess, and petitioned my friend for some emblem of himself which they might install in her stead.

We who are fortunate enough to live in this comparatively enlightened century hardly realize how our ancestors suffered from their belief in the existence of mysterious and malevolent beings; how their life was embittered and overshadowed by these awful apprehensions.

As men, however, have risen in civilization, their religion has risen with them; they have by degrees acquired higher and purer conceptions of divine power.

We are only just beginning to realize that a loving and merciful Father would not resent honest error, not even perhaps the attribution to him of such odious injustice. Yet what can be clearer than Christ's teaching on this point. He impressed it over and over again on his disciples. "The letter killeth, but the spirit giveth life."

"If," says Ruskin, "for every rebuke that we utter of men's vices, we put forth a claim upon their hearts; if, for every assertion of God's demands from them, we should substitute a display of His kindness to them; if side by side, with every warning of death, we could exhibit proofs and promises of immortality; if, in fine, instead of assuming the being of an awful Deity, which men, though they cannot and dare not deny, are always unwilling, sometimes unable, to conceive; we were to show them a near, visible, inevitable, but all-beneficent Deity, whose presence makes the earth itself a heaven, I think there would be fewer deaf children sitting in the market-place."

But it must not be supposed that those who doubt whether the ultimate truth of the Universe can be expressed in human words, or whether, even if it could, we should be able to comprehend it, undervalue the importance of religious study. Quite the contrary. Their doubts arise not from pride, but from humility: not because they do not appreciate divine truth, but on the contrary they doubt whether we can appreciate it sufficiently, and are sceptical whether the infinite can be reduced to the finite.

We may be sure that whatever may be right about religion, to quarrel over it must be wrong. "Let others wrangle," said St. Augustine, "I will wonder."

Those who suspend their judgment are not on that account sceptics, and it is often those who think they know most, who are especially troubled by doubts and anxiety.

It was Wordsworth who wrote

> "Great God, I had rather be
> A Pagan suckled in some creed outworn;
> So might I, standing on this pleasant lea,
> Have glimpses that would make me less forlorn."

In religion, as with children at night, it is darkness and ignorance which create dread; light and love cast out fear.

In looking forward to the future we may fairly hope with Ruskin that "the charities of more and more widely extended peace are preparing the way for a Christian Church which shall depend neither on ignorance for its continuance, nor on controversy for its progress, but shall reign at once in light and love."

CHAPTER XII.
THE HOPE OF PROGRESS.

"To what then may we not look forward, when a spirit of scientific inquiry shall have spread through those vast regions in which the progress of civilization, its sure precursor, is actually commenced and in active progress? And what may we not expect from the exertions of powerful minds called into action under circumstances totally different from any which have yet existed in the world, and over an extent of territory far surpassing that which has hitherto produced the whole harvest of human intellect."

HERSCHEL.

CHAPTER XII.

THE HOPE OF PROGRESS.

THERE are two lines, if not more, in which we may look forward with hope to progress in the future. In the first place, increased knowledge of nature, of the properties of matter, and of the phenomena which surround us, may afford to our children advantages far greater even than those which we ourselves enjoy. Secondly, the extension and improvement of education, the increasing influence of Science and Art, of Poetry and Music, of Literature and Religion,—of all the powers which are tending to good, will, we may reasonably hope, raise man and make him more master of himself, more able to appreciate and enjoy his advantages, and to realize the truth of the Italian proverb, that wherever light is, there is joy.

One consideration which has greatly tended to retard progress has been the floating idea that there was some sort of ingratitude, and even impiety, in attempting to improve on what Divine Providence had arranged for us. Thus Prometheus was said to have incurred the wrath of Jove for bestowing on mortals the use of fire; and other improvements only escaped similar punishment when the ingenuity of priests attributed them to the special favor of some particular deity. This feeling has not even yet quite died out. Even I can remember the time when many excellent persons had a scruple or prejudice against the use of chloroform, because they fancied that pain was ordained under certain circumstances.

We are told that in early Saxon days Edwin, King of Northumbria, called his nobles and his priests around him, to discuss whether a certain missionary should be heard or not. The king was doubtful. At last there rose an old chief, and said:—"You know, O King, how, on a winter evening, when you are sitting at supper in your hall, with your company around you, when the night is dark and dreary, when the rain and the snow rage outside, when the hall inside is lighted and warm with a blazing fire, sometimes it happens that a sparrow flies into the bright hall out of the dark night, flies through the hall and then flies out at the other end into the dark night again. We see him for a few moments, but we know not whence he came nor whither he goes in the blackness of the storm outside. So is the life of man. It appears for a short space in the warmth and brightness of this life, but what came before this life, or what is to follow this life, we know not. If, therefore, these new teachers can enlighten us as to the darkness that went before, and the darkness that is to come after, let us hear what they have to teach us."

It is often said, however, that great and unexpected as recent discoveries have been, there are certain ultimate problems which must ever remain unsolved. For my part, I would prefer to abstain from laying down any such limitations. When Park asked the Arabs what became of the sun at night, and whether the sun was always the same, or new each day, they replied that such a question was foolish, being entirely beyond the reach of human investigation.

M. Comte, in his *Cours de Philosophie Positive*, as recently as 1842, laid it down as an axiom regarding the heavenly bodies, "We may hope to determine their forms, distances, magnitude, and movements, but we shall never by any means be able to study their chemical composition or mineralogical structure." Yet within a few years this supposed impossibility has been actually accomplished, showing how unsafe it is to limit the possibilities of science. [1]

It is, indeed, as true now as in the time of Newton, that the great ocean of truth lies undiscovered before us. I often wish that some President of the Royal Society, or of the British Association, would take for the theme of his annual address "The things we do not know." Who can say on the verge of what discoveries we are perhaps even now standing! It is extraordinary how slight a margin

[1] Lubbock. *Fifty Years of Science.*

may stand for years between Man and some important improvement. Take the case of the electric light, for instance. It had been known for years that if a carbon rod be placed in an exhausted glass receiver, and a current of electricity be passed through it the carbon glowed with an intense light, but on the other hand it became so hot that the glass burst. The light, therefore, was useless, because the lamp burst as soon as it was lighted. Edison hit on the idea that if you made the carbon filament fine enough, you would get rid of the heat and yet have abundance of light. Edison's right to his patent has been contested on this very ground. It has been said that the mere introduction of so small a difference as the replacement of a thin rod by a fine filament was so slight an item that it could not be patented. The improvements by Swan, Lane Fox, and others, though so important as a whole, have been made step by step.

Or take again the discovery of anæsthetics. At the beginning of the century Sir Humphrey discovered laughing gas, as it was then called. He found that it produced complete insensibility to pain and yet did not injure health. A tooth was actually taken out under its influence, and of course without suffering. These facts were known to our chemists, they were explained to the students in our great hospitals, and yet for half a century the obvious application occurred to no one. Operations continued to be performed as before, patients suffered the same horrible tortures, and yet the beneficent element was in our hands, its divine properties were known, but it never occurred to any one to make use of it.

I may give one more illustration. Printing is generally said to have been discovered in the fifteenth century; and so it was for all practical purposes. But in fact printing was known long before. The Romans used stamps; on the monuments of Assyrian kings the name of the reigning monarch may be found duly printed. What then is the difference? One little, but all-important step. The real inventor of printing was the man into whose mind flashed the fruitful idea of having separate stamps for each letter, instead of for separate words. How slight seems the difference, and yet for 3000 years the thought occurred to no one. Who can tell what other discoveries, as simple and yet as far-reaching, lie at this very moment under our very eyes!

Archimedes said that if you would give him room to stand on, he would move the earth. One truth leads to another; each discovery renders possible another, and, what is more, a higher.

We are but beginning to realize the marvelous range and complexity of Nature. I have elsewhere called attention to this with special reference to the problematical organs of sense possessed by many animals.[1]

There is every reason to hope that future studies

[1] *The Senses of Animals.*

will throw much light on these interesting structures. We may, no doubt, expect much from the improvement in our microscopes, the use of new re-agents, and of mechanical appliances; but the ultimate atoms of which matter is composed are so infinitesimally minute, that it is difficult to foresee any manner in which we may hope for a final solution of these problems.

Loschmidt, who has since been confirmed by Stoney and Sir W. Thomson, calculates that each of the ultimate atoms of matter is at most $\frac{1}{50000000}$ of an inch in diameter. Under these circumstances we cannot, it would seem, hope at present for any great increase of our knowledge of atoms by improvements in the microscope. With our present instruments we can perceive lines ruled on glass which are $\frac{1}{90000}$ of an inch apart; but owing to the properties of light itself, it would appear that we cannot hope to be able to perceive objects which are much less than $\frac{1}{10000}$ of an inch in diameter. Our microscopes may, no doubt, be improved, but the limitation lies not in the imperfection of our optical appliances, but in the nature of light itself.

It has been calculated that a particle of albumen $\frac{1}{10000}$ of an inch in diameter contains no less than 125,000,000 of molecules. In a simpler compound the number would be much greater; in water, for instance, no less than 8,000,000,000. Even then, if we could construct microscopes far more powerful than any which we now possess, they could not enable us to obtain by direct vision any idea of the ultimate organization of matter. The smallest sphere of organic matter which could be clearly defined with our most powerful microscopes may be, in reality, very complex; may be built up of many millions of molecules, and it follows that there may be an almost infinite number of structural characters in organic tissues which we can at present foresee no mode of examining.[1]

Again, it has been shown that animals hear sounds which are beyond the range of our hearing, and I have proved they can perceive the ultra-violet rays, which are invisible to our eyes.[2]

Now, as every ray of homogeneous light which we can perceive at all, appears to us as a distinct color, it becomes probable that these ultra-violet rays must make themselves apparent to animals as a distinct and separate color (of which we can form no idea), but as different from the rest as red is from yellow, or green from violet. The question also arises whether white light to these creatures would differ from our white light in containing this additional color.

These considerations cannot but raise the reflection how different the world may—I was going to say must—appear to other animals from what it does to us. Sound is the sensation produced on us when the vibrations of the air strike on the

[1] Lubbock. *Fifty Years of Science.*
[2] *Ants, Bees, and Wasps.*

drum of our ear. When they are few, the sound is deep; as they increase in number, it becomes shriller and shriller; but when they reach 40,000 in a second, they cease to be audible. Light is the effect produced on us when waves of light strike on the eye. When 400 millions of millions of vibrations of ether strike the retina in a second, they produce red, and as the number increases the color passes into orange, then yellow, green, blue, and violet. But between 40,000 vibrations in a second and 400 millions of millions we have no organ of sense capable of receiving the impression. Yet between these limits any number of sensations may exist. We have five senses, and sometimes fancy that no others are possible. But it is obvious that we cannot measure the infinite by our own narrow limitations.

Moreover, looking at the question from the other side, we find in animals complex organs of sense, richly supplied with nerves, but the function of which we are as yet powerless to explain. There may be fifty other senses as different from ours as sound is from sight; and even within the boundaries of our own senses there may be endless sounds which we cannot hear, and colors, as different as red from green, of which we have no conception. These and a thousand other questions remain for solution. The familiar world which surrounds us may be a totally different place to other animals. To them it may be full of music which we cannot hear, of color which we cannot see, of sensations which we cannot conceive. To place stuffed birds and beasts in glass cases, to arrange insects in cabinets, and dried plants in drawers, is merely the drudgery and preliminary of study; to watch their habits, to understand their relations to one another, to study their instincts and intelligence, to ascertain their adaptations and their relations to the forces of Nature, to realize what the world appears to them; these constitute, as it seems to me at least, the true interest of natural history, and may even give us the clue to senses and perceptions of which at present we have no conception.[1]

From this point of view the possibilities of progress seem to me to be almost unlimited.

So far again as the actual condition of man is concerned, the fact that there has been some advance cannot, I think, be questioned.

In the Middle Ages, for instance, culture and refinement scarcely existed beyond the limits of courts, and by no means always there. The life in English, French, and German castles was rough and almost barbarous. Mr. Galton has expressed the opinion, which I am not prepared to question, that the population of Athens, taken as a whole, was as superior to us as we are to Australian savages. But even if that be so, our civilization, such as it is, is more diffused, so that unquestionably the general European level is much higher.

Much, no doubt, is owing to the greater facility

[1] Lubbock. *The Senses of Animals.*

of access to the literature of our country, to that literature, in the words of Macaulay, "the brightest, the purest, the most durable of all the glories of our country; to that Literature, so rich in precious truth and precious fiction; to that Literature which boasts of the prince of all poets, and of the prince of all philosophers; to that Literature which has exercised an influence wider than that of our commerce, and mightier than that of our arms."

Few of us make the most of our minds. The body ceases to grow in a few years; but the mind, if we will let it, may grow as long as life lasts.

The onward progress of the future will not, we may be sure, be confined to mere material discoveries. We feel that we are on the road to higher mental powers; that problems which now seem to us beyond the range of human thought will receive their solution, and open the way to still further advance. Progress, moreover, we may hope, will be not merely material, not merely mental, but moral also.

It is natural that we should feel a pride in the beauty of England, in the size of our cities, the magnitude of our commerce, the wealth of our country, the vastness of our Empire. But the true glory of a nation does not consist in the extent of its dominion, in the fertility of the soil, or the beauty of Nature, but rather in the moral and intellectual pre-eminence of the people.

And yet how few of us, rich or poor, have made ourselves all we might be. If he does his best, as

Shakespeare says, "What a piece of work is man! How noble in reason! How infinite in faculty! in form and movement, how express and admirable!" Few indeed, as yet, can be said to reach this high ideal.

The Hindoos have a theory that after death animals live again in a different form; those that have done well in a higher, those that have done ill in a lower grade. To realize this is, they find, a powerful incentive to a virtuous life. But whether it be true of a future life or not, it is certainly true of our present existence. If we do our best for a day, the next morning we shall rise to a higher life; while if we give way to our passions and temptations, we take with equal certainty a step downward toward a lower nature.

It is an interesting illustration of the Unity of Man, and an encouragement to those of us who have no claims to genius, that, though of course there have been exceptions, still on the whole, periods of progress have generally been those when a nation has worked and felt together; the advance has been due not entirely to the efforts of a few great men, but also of a thousand little men; not to a single genius, but to a national effort.

Think, indeed, what might be.

> "Ah! when shall all men's good
> Be each man's rule, and universal Peace
> Lie like a shaft of light across the land,
> And like a lane of beams athwart the sea,
> Thro' all the circle of the golden year."[1]

[1] Tennyson.

Our life is surrounded with mystery, our very world is a speck in boundless space; and not only the period of our own individual life, but that of the whole human race is, as it were, but a moment in the eternity of time. We cannot imagine any origin, nor foresee the conclusion.

But though we may not as yet perceive any line of research which can give us a clue to the solution, in another sense we may hold that every addition to our knowledge is one small step toward the great revelation.

Progress may be more slow, or more rapid. It may come to others and not to us. It will not come to us if we do not strive to deserve it. But come it surely will.

> "Yet one thing is there that ye shall not slay,
> Even thought, that fire nor iron can affright." [1]

The future of man is full of hope, and who can foresee the limits of his destiny?

[1] Swinburne.

CHAPTER XIII.
THE DESTINY OF MAN.

"For I reckon that the sufferings of this present time are not worthy to be compared with the glory which shall be revealed in us."—ROMANS viii. 18.

CHAPTER XIII.

THE DESTINY OF MAN.

BUT though we have thus a sure and certain hope of progress for the race, still, as far as man is individually concerned, with advancing years we gradually care less and less for many things which gave us the greatest pleasure in youth. On the other hand, if our time has been well used, if we have warmed both hands wisely "before the fire of life," we may gain even more than we lose. If our strength becomes less, we feel also the less necessity for exertion. Hope is gradually replaced by memory: and whether this adds to our happiness or not depends on what our life has been.

There are of course some lives which diminish in value as old age advances, in which one pleasure fades after another, and even those which remain gradually lose their zest; but there are others which gain in richness and peace all, and more, than that of which time robs them.

The pleasures of youth may excel in keenness and in zest, but they have at the best a tinge of anxiety and unrest; they cannot have the fulness and depth which may accompany the consolations of age, and are amongst the richest rewards of an unselfish life.

For as with the close of the day, so with that of life; there may be clouds, and yet if the horizon is clear, the evening may be beautiful.

Old age has a rich store of memories. Life is full of

> " Joys too exquisite to last,
> And yet more exquisite when past." [1]

Swedenborg imagines that in heaven the angels are advancing continually to the spring-time of their youth, so that those who have lived longest are really the youngest; and have we not all had friends who seem to fulfil this idea? who are in reality—that is in mind—as fresh as a child: of whom it may be said with more truth than of Cleopatra that

> " Age cannot wither nor custom stale
> Their infinite variety."

"When I consider old age," says Cicero, "I find four causes why it is thought miserable: one, that it calls us away from the transaction of affairs; the second, that it renders the body more feeble; the third, that it deprives us of almost all pleasures; the fourth, that it is not very far from death. Of these causes let us see, if you please, how great and how reasonable each of them is."

[1] Montgomery.

To be released from the absorbing affairs of life, to feel that one has earned a claim to leisure and repose, is surely in itself no evil.

To the second complaint against old age, I have already referred in speaking of Health.

The third is that it has no passions. "O noble privilege of age! if indeed it takes from us that which is in youth our greatest defect." But the higher feelings of our nature are not necessarily weakened; or rather, they may become all the brighter, being purified from the grosser elements of our lower nature.

Then, indeed, it might be said that "Man is the sun of the world; more than the real sun. The fire of his wonderful heart is the only light and heat worth gauge or measure."[1]

"Single," says Manu, "is each man born into the world; single he dies; single he receives the rewards of his good deeds; and single the punishment of his sins. When he dies his body lies like a fallen tree upon the earth, but his virtue accompanies his soul. Wherefore let Man harvest and garner virtue, that so he may have an inseparable companion in that gloom which all must pass through, and which it is so hard to traverse."

Is it not extraordinary that many men will deliberately take a road which they know is, to say the least, not that of happiness? That they prefer to make others miserable, rather than themselves happy?

[1] Emerson.

Plato, in the Phædrus, explains this by describing Man as a Composite Being, having three natures, and compares him to a pair of winged horses and a charioteer. "Of the two horses one is noble and of noble origin, the other ignoble and of ignoble origin; and the driving, as might be expected, is no easy matter." The noble steed endeavors to raise the chariot, but the ignoble one struggles to drag it down.

"Man," says Shelly, "is an instrument over which a series of external and internal impressions are driven, like the alternations of an ever-changing wind over an Æolian lyre, which move it by their motion to ever-changing melody."

Cicero mentions the approach of death as the fourth drawback of old age. To many minds the shadow of the end is ever present, like the coffin in the Egyptian feast, and overclouds all the sunshine of life. But ought we so to regard death?

Shelly's beautiful lines,

> "Life, like a Dome of many-colored glass,
> Stains the white radiance of Eternity,
> Until death tramples it to fragments,"

contain, as it seems to me at least, a double error. Life need not stain the white radiance of eternity; nor does death necessarily trample it to fragments.

Man has, says Coleridge,

> "Three treasures,—love and light
> And calm thoughts, regular as infants' breath;
> And three firm friends, more sure than day and night,
> Himself, his Maker, and the Angel Death."

Death is "the end of all, the remedy of many, the wish of divers men, deserving better of no men than of those to whom she came before she was called."[1]

It is often assumed that the journey to

> "The undiscovered country from whose bourne
> No traveler returns"

must be one of pain and suffering. But this is not so. Death is often peaceful and almost painless.

Bede during his late illness was translating St. John's Gospel into Anglo-Saxon, and the morning of his death his secretary, observing his weakness, said, "There remains now only one chapter, and it seems difficult to you to speak." "It is easy," said Bede; "take your pen and write as fast as you can." At the close of the chapter the scribe said, "It is finished," to which he replied, "Thou hast said the truth, *consummatum est.*" He then divided his little property among the brethren, having done which he asked to be placed opposite to the place where he usually prayed, said "Glory be to the Father, and to the Son, and to the Holy Ghost," and as he pronounced the last words he expired.

[1] Seneca.

Goethe died without any apparent suffering, having just prepared himself to write, and expressed his delight at the return of spring.

We are told of Mozart's death that "the unfinished requiem lay upon the bed, and his last efforts were to imitate some peculiar instrumental effects, as he breathed out his life in the arms of his wife and their friend Süssmaier."

Plato died in the act of writing; Lucan while reciting part of his book on the war of Pharsalus; Blake died singing; Wagner in sleep with his head on his wife's shoulder. Many have passed away in their sleep. Various high medical authorities have expressed their surprise that the dying seldom feel either dismay or regret. And even those who perish by violence, as for instance in battle, feel, it is probable, but little suffering.

But what of the future? There may be said to be now two principal views. There are some who believe indeed in the immortality of the soul, but not of the individual soul: that our life is continued in that of our children would seem indeed to be the natural deduction from the simile of St. Paul, as that of the grain of wheat is carried on in the plant of the following year.

So long indeed as happiness exists it is selfish to dwell too much on our own share in it. Admit that the soul is immortal, but that in the future state of existence there is a break in the continuity of memory, that one does not remember the present life, and from this point of view is not the importance of identity involved in that of continuous memory? But however this may be according to the general view, the soul, though detached from the body, will retain its conscious identity, and will awake from death, as it does from sleep; so that if we cannot affirm that

"Millions of spiritual creatures walk the Earth,
Unseen, both when we wake, and when we sleep,"[1]

at any rate they exist somewhere else in space, and we are indeed looking at them when we gaze at the stars, though to our eyes they are as yet invisible.

In neither case, however, can death be regarded as an evil. To wish that youth and strength were unaffected by time might be a different matter.

"But if we are not destined to be immortal, yet it is a desirable thing for a man to expire at his fit time. For, as nature prescribes a boundary to all other things, so does she also to life. Now old age is the consummation of life, just as of a play: from the fatigue of which we ought to escape, especially when satiety is super-added."[2]

From this point of view, then, we need

"Weep not for death,
  'Tis but a fever stilled,
A pain suppressed,—a fear at rest,
  A solemn hope fulfilled.
The moonshine on the slumbering deep
Is scarcely calmer. Wherefore weep?

[1] Milton. [2] Cicero.

> "Weep not for death!
>   The fount of tears is sealed,
>   Who knows how bright the inward light
>   To those closed eyes revealed?
>   Who knows what holy love may fill
>   The heart that seems so cold and still."

Many a weary soul will have recurred with comfort to the thought that

> "A few more years shall roll,
>   A few more seasons come,
>   And we shall be with those that rest
>   Asleep within the tomb.
>
> "A few more struggles here,
>   A few more partings o'er,
>   A few more toils, a few more tears,
>   And we shall weep no more."

By no one has this, however, been more grandly expressed than by Shelley.

> "Peace, peace! he is not dead, he doth not sleep!
>   He hath awakened from the dream of life.
>   'Tis we who, lost in stormy visions, keep
>   With phantoms an unprofitable strife,
>   He has outsoared the shadows of our night.
>   Envy and calumny, and hate and pain,
>   And that unrest which men miscall delight,
>   Can touch him not and torture not again.
>   From the contagion of the world's slow stain
>   He is secure, and now can never mourn
>   A heart grown cold, a head grown gray, in vain—"

Most men, however, decline to believe that

> "We are such stuff
> As dreams are made of, and our little life
> Is rounded with a sleep."[1]

According to the more general view death frees the soul from the encumbrance of the spirit, and summons us to the seat of judgment. In fact,

> "There is no Death! What seems so is transition;
> This life of mortal breath
> Is but a suburb of the life elysian,
> Whose portal we call Death."[2]

We have bodies, "we are spirits." "I am a soul," said Epictetus, "dragging about a corpse." The body is the mere perishable form of the immortal essence. Plato concluded that if the ways of God are to be justified, there must be a future life.

To the aged in either case death is a release. The Bible dwells most forcibly on the blessing of peace. "My peace I give unto you: not as the world giveth, give I unto you." Heaven is described as a place where the wicked cease from troubling, and the weary are at rest.

But I suppose every one must have asked himself in what can the pleasures of heaven consist.

> "For all we know
> Of what the blessed do above
> Is that they sing, and that they love."[3]

[1] Shakespeare.   [2] Longfellow.   [3] Waller.

It would indeed accord with few men's ideal that there should be any "struggle for existence" in heaven. We should then be little better off than we are now. This world is very beautiful, if we could only enjoy it in peace. And yet mere passive existence—mere vegetation—would in itself offer few attractions. It would indeed be almost intolerable.

Again, the anxiety of change seems inconsistent with perfect happiness; and yet a wearisome, interminable monotony, the same thing over and over again forever and ever without relief or variety, suggests dulness rather than bliss.

I feel that to me, said Greg, "God has promised not the heaven of the ascetic temper, or the dogmatic theologian, or of the subtle mystic, or of the stern martyr ready alike to inflict and bear; but a heaven of purified and permanent affections —of a book of knowledge with eternal leaves, and unbounded capacities to read it—of those we love ever round us, never misconceiving us, or being harassed by us—of glorious work to do, and adequate faculties to do it—a world of solved problems, as well as of realized ideals."

"For still the doubt came back,—Can God provide
   For the large heart of man what shall not pall,
Nor through eternal ages' endless tide
   On tired spirits fall?

"These make him say,—If God has so arrayed
   A fading world that quickly passes by,
Such rich provision of delight has made
   For every human eye,

> What shall the eyes that wait for him survey
>   When his own presence gloriously appears
> In worlds that were not founded for a day,
>   But for eternal years?" [1]

Here science seems to suggest a possible answer: the solution of problems which have puzzled us here; the acquisition of new ideas; the unrolling the history of the past; the world of animals and plants; the secrets of space; the wonders of the stars and of the regions beyond the stars. To become acquainted with all the beautiful and interesting spots of our own world would indeed be something to look forward to, and our world is but one of many millions. I sometimes wonder as I look away to the stars at night whether it will ever be my privilege as a disembodied spirit to visit and explore them. When we had made the great tour fresh interests would have arisen, and we might well begin again.

Here there is an infinity of interest without anxiety. So that at last the only doubt may be

> "Lest an eternity should not suffice
>   To take the measure and the breadth and height
> Of what there is reserved in Paradise
>   Its ever-new delight." [2]

Cicero surely did not exaggerate when he said, "O glorious day! when I shall depart to that divine company and assemblage of spirits, and quit

[1] Trench. [2] Trench.

this troubled and polluted scene. For I shall go not only to those great men of whom I have spoken before, but also to my son Cato, than whom never was better man born, nor more distinguished for pious affection; whose body was burned by me, whereas, on the contrary, it was fitting that mine should be burned by him. But his soul not deserting me, but oft looking back, no doubt departed to these regions whither it saw that I myself was destined to come. Which, though a distress to me, I seemed patiently to endure: not that I bore it with indifference, but I comforted myself with the recollection that the separation and distance between us would not continue long. For these reasons, O Scipio (since you said that you with Lælius were accustomed to wonder at this), old age is tolerable to me, and not only not irksome, but even delightful. And if I am wrong in this, that I believe the souls of men to be immortal, I willingly delude myself: nor do I desire that this mistake, in which I take pleasure, should be wrested from me as long as I live; but if I, when dead, shall have no consciousness, as some narrow-minded philosophers imagine, I do not fear lest dead philosophers should ridicule this my delusion.''

Nor can I omit the striking passage in the *Apology*, when pleading before the people of Athens, Socrates says, ''Let us reflect in another way, and we shall see that there is great reason to hope that death is a good; for one of two things —either death is a state of nothingness and utter unconsciousness, or, as men say, there is a change and migration of the soul from this world to another. Now if you suppose that there is no consciousness, but a sleep like the sleep of him who is undisturbed even by the sight of dreams, death will be an unspeakable gain. For if a person were to select the night in which his sleep was undisturbed even by dreams, and were to compare with this the other days and nights of his life, and then were to tell us how many days and nights he had passed in the course of his life better and more pleasantly than this one, I think that any man, I will not say a private man, but even the great king will not find many such days or nights, when compared with the others. Now, if death is like this, I say that to die is gain; for eternity is then only a single night. But if death is the journey to another place, and there, as men say, all the dead are, what good, O my friends and judges, can be greater than this?

"If, indeed, when the pilgrim arrives in the world below, he is delivered from the professors of justice in this world, and finds the true judges, who are said to give judgment there,—Minos, and Rhadamanthus, and Æacus, and Triptolemus, and other sons of God who were righteous in their own life,—that pilgrimage will be worth making. What would not a man give if he might converse with Orpheus, and Musæus, and Hesiod, and Homer? Nay, if this be true, let me die again and again. I myself, too, shall have a wonderful interest in there meeting and conversing with Palamedes, and Ajax the son of Telamon, and other heroes of old, who have suffered death through an unjust judgment; and there will be no small pleasure, as I think, in comparing my own sufferings with theirs. Above all, I shall then be able to continue my search into true and false knowledge; as in this world, so also in that; and I shall find out who is wise, and who pretends to be wise, and is not. What would not a man give, O judges, to be able to examine the leader of the great Trojan expedition; or Odysseus or Sisyphus, or numberless others, men and women too! What infinite delight would there be in conversing with them and asking them questions. In another world they do not put a man to death for asking questions; assuredly not. For besides being happier in that world than in this, they will be immortal, if what is said be true.

"Wherefore, O judges, be of good cheer about death, and know of a certainty that no evil can happen to a good man, either in life or after death. He and his are not neglected by the gods; nor has my own approaching end happened by mere chance. But I see clearly that to die and be released was better for me; and therefore the oracle gave no sign. For which reason, also, I am not angry with my condemners, or with my accusers; they have done me no harm, although they did not mean to do me any good; and for this I may gently blame them. The hour of departure has arrived, and we go our ways—I to die and you to live. Which is better God only knows."

In the *Wisdom of Solomon* we are promised that—

" The souls of the righteous are in the hand of God, and there shall no torment touch them.

" In the sight of the unwise they seemed to die ; and their departure is taken for misery.

" And their going from us to be utter destruction ; but they are in peace.

" For though they be punished in the sight of men, yet is their hope full of immortality.

" And having been a little chastised, they shall be greatly rewarded : for God proved them, and found them worthy for himself."

And assuredly, if in the hour of death the conscience is at peace, the mind need not be troubled. The future is full of doubt, indeed, but fuller still of hope.

If we are entering upon a rest after the struggles of life,

" Where the wicked cease from troubling,
And the weary are at rest, "

that to many a weary soul will be a welcome bourne, and even then we may say,

" O Death! where is thy sting ?
O Grave! where is thy victory ? "

On the other hand, if we are entering on a new

sphere of existence, where we may look forward to meet not only those of whom we have heard so often, those whose works we have read and admired, and to whom we owe so much, but those also whom we have loved and lost; when we shall leave behind us the bonds of the flesh and the limitations of our earthly existence; when we shall join the Angels, and Archangels, and all the company of Heaven,—then, indeed, we may cherish a sure and certain hope that the interests and pleasures of this world are as nothing compared to those of the life that awaits us in our Eternal Home.

THE END.

The Altemus Library.

A choice collection of Standard and Popular books, handsomely printed on fine paper, from large clear type, and bound in faultless styles in handy volume size:

1. Sesame and Lilies. 3 Lectures. By John Ruskin.
   I. Of King's Treasuries.
   II. Of Queen's Gardens.
   III. Of the Mystery of Life.
2. The Pleasures of Life. By Sir John Lubbock. Complete in one volume. (Contains the list of *The 100 Best Books*.)
3. The Essays of Lord Francis Bacon, with Memoirs and Notes.
4. Thoughts of the Emperor Marcus Aurelius Antoninus. Translated by George Long.
5. A Selection from the Discourses of Epictetus, with the Encheridion. Translated by George Long.
6. Essays, *First Series*. By Ralph Waldo Emerson.
7. Essays, *Second Series*. By Ralph Waldo Emerson.
8. Cranford. By Mrs Gaskell.
9. Of the Imitation of Christ. Four books complete in one volume. By Thomas A'Kempis.
10. The Vicar of Wakefield. By Oliver Goldsmith.
11. Letters, Sentences and Maxims. By Lord Chesterfield. "Masterpieces of good taste, good writing, and good sense."
12. The Idle Thoughts of an Idle Fellow. A book for an Idle Holiday. By Jerome K. Jerome.
13. Tales from Shakespeare. By Charles and Mary Lamb, with an introduction by Rev. Alfred Ainger, M. A.

The Altemus Library.

14. Natural Law in the Spiritual World. By Henry Drummond, F. R. S. E., F. G. S. The relations of Science and Religion clearly expounded.
15. Addresses. By Henry Drummond, F. R. S. E., F. G. S. The Greatest Thing in the World; Pax Vobiscum; The Changed Life; How to Learn How; Dealing with Doubt; Preparation for Learning; What is a Christian? The Study of the Bible; A Talk on Books.
16. "My Point of View." Representative selections from the works of Professor Drummond. By William Shepard.
17. The Scarlet Letter. By Nathaniel Hawthorne.
18. Representative Men. Seven lectures. By Ralph Waldo Emerson.
19. My King and His Service. By Frances Ridley Havergal. Containing—My King; Royal Commandments; Royal Bounty; Royal Invitation; Loyal Responses.
20. Reveries of a Bachelor. By Ik Marvel. A Book of the Heart.
21. The House of the Seven Gables. By Nathaniel Hawthorne.
22. Dream Life. By Ik Marvel. A Companion volume to Reveries of a Bachelor.
23. Rab and His Friends, Marjorie Fleming, etc. By John Brown.
24. Essays of Elia. By Charles Lamb.
25. Sartor Resartus. By Thomas Carlyle.
26. Heroes and Hero Worship. By Thomas Carlyle.

The Altemus Library.

27. Ethics of the Dust. By John Ruskin.
28. A Window in Thrums. By J. M. Barrie.
29. Mosses from an Old Manse. By Nathaniel Hawthorne.
30. Twice-Told Tales. By Nathaniel Hawthorne.
31. Uncle Tom's Cabin. By Harriet Beecher Stowe.
32. The Sketch Book. By Washington Irving.
33. Greek Heroes. By Charles Kingsley.
34. Undine. By De La Motte Fouqué.
35. A Wonder Book. By Nathaniel Hawthorne.
36. Balzac's Shorter Stories.
37. Two Years Before the Mast. By R. H. Dana, Jr.
38. Autobiography of Benjamin Franklin.
39. Weird Tales. By Edgar Allan Poe.
40. The Crown of Wild Olive. By John Ruskin.
41. Tom Brown's School Days. By Thomas Hughes.

Cloth, various handsome designs stamped in gold and silver, ... 75 cents.

Half-crushed levant, super-extra hand-finished, gold tops, untrimmed edges, sewn with silk, . $1.50.

Half-genuine English calf, super-extra hand-finished, gold tops, untrimmed edges, sewn with silk, . $2.00.

HENRY ALTEMUS, Publisher, Philadelphia

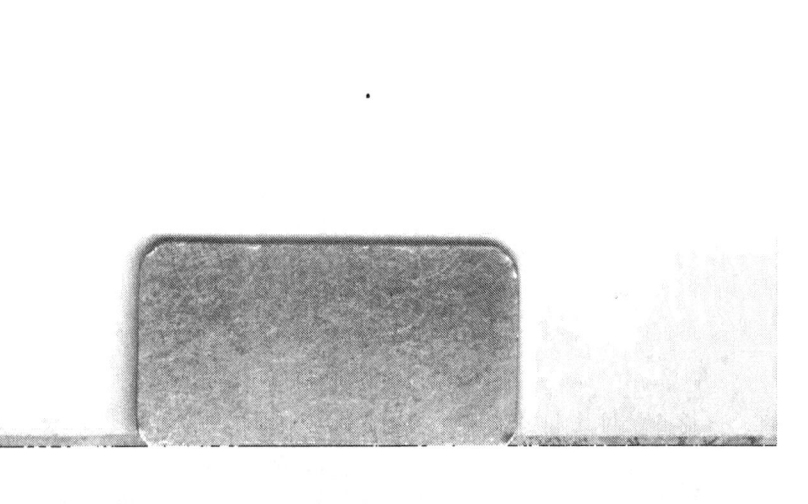